297/3022

636.
10092
ANS.

Moreton Morrell Site

D1146377

Leopard —
The Story of my Horse

WITHDRAWN

Warwickshire College

00522270

WARWICKSHIRE COLLEGE LIBRARY

By the same author —

SOLDIER ON
RIDING HIGH

LEOPARD —

The Story of my Horse

COLONEL
SIR MICHAEL ANSELL, CBE, DSO

Warwickshire College
Library
Moreton Morrell Centre

Class No: 636.10092

Acc No: 00500270

Quartilles International Limited
Coggeshall, Essex

First published 1980
© Colonel Sir Michael Ansell

All rights reserved. No part of this publication may be reproduced, stored in a retrieval system, or transmitted in any form or by any means, electronic, mechanical, photocopying, recording or otherwise, without the prior permission of Quartilles International Limited.

**Warwickshire College
Library
Moreton Morrell Centre**

Class No: 636. 10092

Acc No: 00522270

Printed and bound in Great Britain by
KNAPP DREWETT & SONS LTD.
Kingston upon Thames, Surrey
For Quartilles International Limited
30 West Street, Coggeshall, Colchester, Essex CO6 1NS

This book is set in 11pt Baskerville

ISBN 0 903021 17 X

FRONTISPIECE — From the painting "Cooling Streams" by the late Gilbert Holiday.

ACKNOWLEDGEMENTS

My thanks as always to Denis Goacher who has worked closely with me on this my third book. Mrs. Williams, my sister, and indeed all my family have been unsparingly helpful, re-reading to me at various stages. I am indebted to Ronald Duncan for his expert advice.

My gratitude to Hermione Wynn who has wonderfully maintained her enthusiasm checking and sifting facts through documents, letters, tape recordings, etc.

Details of my hunting, racing and ever happy Regimental life have been most kindly verified by the late Stanley Barker, Kennel Huntsman of the Middleton and subsequently Huntsman of the Pytchley; by Mr. Anthony Preston, M.F.H. York and Ainsty; Mr. Tom Walls, once a Subaltern in my Regiment, whose famous father trained Leopard for his first race; and the indefatigable Miss Biddy Shennan who spent much time tracing the pedigree of Leopard's sire, Maître Corbeau.

I could never forget Trooper Peat and all those who looked after my horse, nor our Farrier Major Gus Newport who first branded him C 29 and whose meticulous care was vindicated by the fact that Leopard never once lost a shoe.

I am also indebted to Generals Sir John Anderson and Sir Cecil Blacker, who, Subalterns in Leopard's day, would be among the first to agree how much we all learned from looking after such horses.

Lieut. Colonel W. A. Evans, now commanding the

Royal Inniskilling Dragoon Guards has kindly allowed me to reproduce the incomparable drawings of the late Gilbert Holiday, and the late Miss W. Roberts, both great personal friends. *The Field* has extended me the same courtesy for certain drawings.

Finally, but only by position on the page, I must thank Captain C. J. Boardman, who searched for photographs and other historical records, and Mr. A. C. Littlejohns, of Bideford, for his advice and help in the reproduction of the illustrations.

CONTENTS

LIST OF PHOTOGRAPHS
AND ILLUSTRATIONS

FOREWORD
by
**H.R.H. Prince Charles
Prince of Wales, K.G.**

For thousands of years the lives of men and of horses have been inextricably entwined — from Alexander The Great and Bucephalus, to Wellington and Copenhagen and, in our own day, to such a partnership as Pat Taaffe and Arkle. There can surely be no partnership quite like that which exists between man and horse — that curious kind of mutual respect and understanding which, if you are lucky, can lead to extraordinary feats of skill, endurance and courage.

All those whose lives revolve, to any extent, around horses will appreciate only too well the joys, the exhilaration and, of course, the frustrations that they can provide. Even those whose lives are not directly involved with horses cannot, I feel sure, fail to be moved and stirred by Sir Mike Ansell's wonderful account of his famous horse, Leopard. For me it is the most romantic of ideas that such a unique horse should have been spotted by the veterinary surgeon of the Inniskilling Dragoon Guards while he was riding past the camp site of a Welsh tinker in the wilds of Yorkshire. The whole thing seems so unlikely and yet this man's eye for a horse proved only too true and in Mike Ansell's sympathetic and brilliant hands Leopard turned into everything that a man could possibly hope for in a horse.

As someone who rather easily becomes sentimentally attached to a horse, I must admit that I was moved to tears of exhilaration and sympathy by the way in which Mike Ansell describes Leopard. Not only is this a touching story of the relationship that can grow between a man and his horse, but it is also a fascinating and nostalgic insight into the life of a cavalry regiment between the two world wars. Reading about the daily routine of a trooper or a cavalry officer in the 1930's emphasizes the great changes which have taken place in a comparatively short space of time. Gone for instance, is that elusive sense of innocence which somehow seemed to pervade the years before the era of mass mechanized transportation and sophisticated methods of communication.

The horse, in a curious way, helps us to keep closer to Nature; to be aware of those things around us which otherwise we might miss through being artificially cut off from them in the course of our increasingly complex and sophisticated lives. The story of Leopard, however, will always be there to remind us of that unique bond which can exist between a sympathetic human being and an animal and will never fail to inspire us, to fill us with nostalgic sentiment and will probably make us cry in the end. I am sure everyone who reads this will wish they had a horse like him — I wish I did!

INTRODUCTION

In the Army Quarterly of October 1937 some 30 famous cavalry horses were picked out from the cavalry's three hundred years' history. Of these thirty horses, twenty-nine achieved fame on the battlefield and the thirtieth, *Leopard,* came to the fore at a time when the mounted cavalry was fast disappearing and the Cavalry Regiments were being mechanised.

"One of the most famous horses of the 'early days' was *'The Byerley Turk'* an Arabian bay charger from whom, together with two other Eastern sires, all English thoroughbreds are descended. Before being put to the stud on the Colonel's retirement, for he was imported by Colonel Robert Byerley of the Carabiniers in 1689, he acquitted himself well as a charger and had it not been for his remarkable speed his master would most assuredly have been captured when galloping too far forward at the Battle of the Boyne, where the Inniskillings and the 5th Dragoon Guards fought side by side."

"At the Charge of the Light Brigade at Balaclava, Lord Cardigan led the immortal Six Hundred on his chestnut charger *'Ronald'*, who survived the charge and died a natural death some years later. Wellington's chestnut *'Copenhagen'* is well-known, having led the forces to victory at Waterloo. This horse lived until he was 28. Many of the cavalry horses were famous for their own individual tricks.

One of these was '*Casey*', the charger ridden by General Archie Macdonnell who, before becoming a Divisional Commander, commanded Lord Strathcona's Horse. *Casey's* most famous trick was that of lying down and pretending to be dead, Macdonnell would then bend down and whisper in his ear 'The Kaiser'. That immediately brought *Casey* up on his legs again. Also we must not forget the drum horses who are so attractive and must be strong to carry a man and a pair of kettle drums."

"*Leopard* was a horse who became famous in spite of the fact that horses were fast disappearing from the British Army. This remarkable cavalry charger was bought as a remount when tied to a tinker's cart at York and under the tuition of the author, a Captain of the 5th Inniskilling Dragoon Guards, developed into a show jumper, hunter and steeplechase winner. *Leopard* was also to the fore at dummy thrusting, and could jump any fence without bridle or reins. It was for the special benefit of King George V that *Leopard* once gave a private performance without bridle in the riding school at Aldershot. His jumping feat used to be one of the main features of the riding display carried out by the Regiment at the major shows."

Apart from telling the story of this great horse, I've been concerned with paying tribute, from a very personal angle, to a moment in history which went largely unsung: the end of the use of horses in war.

The paradox is this: had I not been trained for the cavalry I should in no sense be what I am or think, and feel as I do. Yet, I am profoundly grateful that neither *Leopard* nor any of my horses went to war. A contradiction; life teems with contradictions: that is what life is.

CHAPTER 1
A new recruit

Once upon a time, for that is the way we have to begin, Cavalry meant what it said and there weren't any wheels. We served overseas for seven years or more, on India's North West Frontier and even beyond, and then we came home for a rest. York was our billet in 1927 and the Inniskilling Dragoon Guards thought themselves fortunate: foggy York was damp, but the Mecca for cavalry regiments returning from overseas — here we could recuperate and reorganise.

All of us enjoyed York's social life, some of us could hunt. That more than anything taught us our trade — horsemastership and horsemanship — and therefore mastery of our art, while constantly, incessantly, developing an eye for the country. Hunting teaches a soldier what to expect, what to avoid, and when to take a risk.

Our life was not leisurely, though now many say it was. Simply, life seemed to have more space and time then, people did different things. It is stupid to talk of privilege just because your soldier-groom might be sent ahead to the meet with the horses, while the young officer fulfilled his military duties in the barracks. Then a quick change and off to the meet in a rather old motor car. At the end of a long and happy day, a twenty mile ride home over roads well-gritted but not overburdened with lorries and other monsters bearing down on you with blazing lights.

I realise that the times and the landscape are now so changed that I might be telling you a tale of the Middle Ages, yet it's less than fifty years ago. Perhaps there's some value in fixing these memories of what actually happened. Soon those days will be regarded as a myth. Perhaps they are already?

Early one evening in the first days of that January, Adam, the Inniskillings' excellent veterinary surgeon, rode home quietly through the twilight. It had been a good hunt, ending on the Wolds near Birdsall. Without thinking he took the old road past Aldby Park, a splendid Georgian building which housed the Master of the Middleton Hounds — Colonel 'Peach' Borwick, ex-cavalry officer of the Scots Greys.

Adam was an Irishman and therefore a great judge of horses. As he approached Aldby over the hills, past the small fields with their thick thorn fences — what superb country that was — in the half light he saw first a small fire burning, and a tent nearby and a tinker's cart. In the field were three horses, they looked thin, cold and forlorn. But after all it was January.

One of the three, a chestnut colt, immediately pricked up his ears and trotted over to greet the sound of hooves on the road. Even in the dusk Adam was, at once, impressed by the way the young colt moved and he called over to the tinker hunched beside the fire while his wife bustled around cooking the evening meal.

'Mister, what is that chestnut colt?'

'He's a real beauty although a bit on the light side, mark you,' replied the tinker, obviously a Welshman.

'What are you doing with these three horses then?' enquired Adam.

'Well now,' said Dave (for that was his name), 'one, the old mare, takes us around the country, the colt is just four years old, the bay three, and if I want to sell a horse I come to Yorkshire, the finest "horse" county in the world.'

More and more Adam liked the way that colt moved. Desperately thin, but there was something about him.

'Where did you get this chestnut?'

6

'Out of my old mare, but I was lucky the stallion was *Maître Corbeau.*'

Adam was authorised to buy horses for the army, up to a limit of £40.

'Do you want to sell him?'

'Not arf' chirped Dave, 'that is why I come to this county.'

'I will see you tomorrow but are you sure he's by *Maître Corbeau?*

'Oh yes, for he's out of my mare who fostered a foal of *Maître Corbeau* in Glamorgan, and in return the master allowed my old mare a free service.'

'I'll be seeing you in the morning, good night.' And away jogged Adam into the dusk.

Later that evening, in the Fulford Barracks, he searched through his books with more than usual interest. Yes, sure enough there he was; *Maître Corbeau,* black stallion, born in Ireland, not much success racing. Possibly because he'd broken down or become lame Wickham-Boynton had bought him for the Burton Agnes Stud. Then from the Yorkshire Wolds the stallion had been sold to a small stud in Glamorgan. Adam wasn't satisfied, his nose scented something more and he searched until he delightedly discovered that the dam side of *Maître Corbeau* listed *Hermit,* a winner of the Derby many years before. That clinched the matter.

Next morning, at eight sharp, Adam rode the seven miles to Aldby where Dave had packed up and was just putting the old mare between the shafts.

'Here I am, as promised, let's have another look at that chestnut colt, if you please.'

Being short of cash Dave was only too pleased — even in those days it cost a bit to keep a horse.

The colt stood 16.2 hands high and Adam was quite impressed by the way he moved at the walk and the trot.

'Well now, Dave, how much do you want for him if the Army will buy him?'

'Forty quid' (our Dave knew only too well the top price for a troop horse).

'Not likely, look at his ribs, though I might give you

7

twenty and another five for luck.'

Dave pretended to calculate hard, but the issue wasn't in doubt — 'All right guv', he simply said, looking very philosophical.

So the tinker broke camp and set his cart on the road south west and Adam rode off, leading the chestnut colt another way through the woods and after a minute or two he realised the sun was shining very bright — that peculiar steely brilliance we sometimes get in early months of the English year. Adam thought how curious it was that this son of *Maître Corbeau* should come back to Yorkshire where his

"So the Tinker broke camp."

1.

sire had stood at stud, and remembered from the records how the black stallion had died, somewhat tragically, from sunstroke. He didn't see the irony of that for Adam felt happy and quite pleased with himself as he entered the barracks, the thin colt jogging beside him, the hard white light staring down at them.

The evening of that same day Adam came up to me in the Mess. 'I've a horse for you, but keep quiet about it, he's so thin and miserable no one will want him.'

In the cavalry regiments of those distant times there were many rituals, one of them was: all young horses (known as remounts) went first to the veterinary stables for three weeks' quarantine. Having been proved clear of the strangles, and other diseases, on such and such a day twenty or so of them were brought to the square and led around to be viewed by the Squadron Leaders. Each of the four Squadron Leaders then drew to decide the order of choice. Each had some of his junior officers with him and the Squadron Sergeant Major too. My squadron leader's initials happened to be H.O.W., naturally he was called 'How' and his S.S.M., a really huge old soldier, was named Tennuci. All S.S.M.s detested these horses — how could skeletons win what was termed the 'fat' horse competition? — and were always looking for horses that would keep fat, fit and well on a small ration.

I stood beside 'How' Wylie and having been cunningly briefed by Adam, said, 'Sir, if you draw first would you please pick that thin chestnut?'

Sergeant Major Tennuci drew in his breath and became so red I thought he was going to throw a fit, but 'How' (he was too aptly named being infinitely wily) knew the right way to coax and when Tennuci had regained something of his normal colour How turned to me: — 'Right, but if I do get him for C Squadron he's to go straight to your own stable and mind he looks well!'

From then on, everything happened as I knew it would. The draw made, 'How' Wylie was first, and to everyone's bewilderment he chose a rather miserable chestnut colt. No one saw Adam smile contentedly and certainly no one knew how much I'd learned from Adam.

We all have stories of premonitions, but as that colt was walked off, a little stiffly but elegantly, first to the farrier's shop to be branded C 29 on his hoof and then to my stable, I knew that this chestnut, with the delicate grey and dark spots would do something unusual. At that moment of branding the young recruit C 29, little did Gus Newport realise what a big part he would play in this horse's life, whether it was racing, hunting, show jumping or carrying out his military duties.

This horse reminded me of one of those unknown princes who used to appear at mediaeval tournaments. I wasn't far wrong, for my lovely horse performed before the admiring eyes of three monarchs.

Fulford Barracks were old, cold and damp. Yet even on chilly mornings, wrapped in that particularly yellow fog, all was warmth and friendliness after the excessive heat and the rigours of the North West Frontier.

The 5th Inniskilling Dragoon Guards were what was known as a Divisional Cavalry Regiment. There were five in Great Britain at that time. Just under 300 horses on the strength and about 450 men. Every officer's first thought was for his horses, and then for his men. I hope no 'progressive' will be humourless about that — the men were certainly not hard done by — but a horseman cannot exist without his horse.

Around a black damp square, barrack rooms and stables were grouped. The buildings uniformly ugly though their prominence had recently been stolen by new latrines, standing up smartly in their white limewash. Four main blocks, one to each squadron, and the horses were housed on the ground floor while the men slept in rooms above the stables. This system provided more warmth for the horses and obviously for the men, as heat rises, but doubtless a modern sanitary inspector would disapprove.

A troop stable took about twenty horses, each fastened in his stall by a rope through a ring to a round log, giving him freedom to lie down. The horses were separated by long iron bars, known as bale bars. The officers had similar troop stables but they usually erected loose boxes in them so these horses were more comfortable.

On that January day C 29 was led to Mr. Ansell's stable to be greeted by my friend and soldier groom, Trooper Peat, a round faced Yorkshireman. Peat was a picked man, and needed to be, for I'd just returned from the Equitation School at Weedon to take charge of remounts and young recruits.

'Come on old boy,' growled Peat, 'goodness, you've been a bit short of grub but we'll soon put that right.' Trooper Peat took over C 29's rope, leading him to the loose box from which he would now look across that black tarmac square.

C 29 shook himself slightly, sniffed and proceeded to survey these odd surroundings. Next door stood a dark brown with above his name, *Pilot* on a smartly painted board, and beyond a bright chestnut, *Flying Fish*. Champions these, obviously, for under the name boards shone glass cases full of prize rosettes. Who was this on the other side with a longish coat, in the rough, as we say? It was *Cuthbert* with other polo ponies, resting during the winter months.

10

Meanwhile, Trooper Peat had been having a real good look at him: 'You're all right my lad, but you bin 'arf starved.' The ration per day per horse was 3 lbs of bran, 8 lbs of oats, 15 lbs of hay or chaff. But Peat hadn't been a squadron forage orderly for nothing. He knew well how to save on one horse, a good doer, in order to give such as C 29 a bit extra.

At this time I was blessed with three soldier grooms although only two were officially allowed. As Equitation Officer it was essential to have a full stable. I never seemed to stop. Even after a day's hunting I often took a young horse to the indoor riding school and worked him quietly on my own. Such was the case on this particular evening. Peat waited around for my return but Troopers Luxford and Turnbull filed off to York to enjoy themselves.

Dark came to the stables. One or two horses muzzled up to each other over the low doors, exchanging their silent messages. Lights at intervals about the bleak square, brightest up by the Main Gate where the Guard for the night was falling in. Wonderfully smart they were too, in riding pants, puttees and spurs, each with a white belt and drawn sword. Would those ever be used again? Apart from this Main Guard we had a large Stable Guard, four men to each squadron, four of whom, one from each squadron, would move quietly round the stables for two hours, then four hours rest before being roused by the N.C.O. to take over for a second term of duty. These chaps looked equally immaculate in carefully pressed slacks with overcoat rolled and slung over the right shoulder, and one of the three carried a highly burnished oil lantern. A lantern? In days when all stables had electric light? It had to be a lantern so as not to wake the horses.

The Guard had just finished their first inspection when I slowly came back to find Peat — deep in conversation with this new colt. Peat loved horses as a mother and had just as much intuitive understanding. Who can say what it meant to such a man when armour prevailed and horses were banned from this rôle for ever? When Trooper Peat, commanding a tank, won the Military Medal for gallantry in Normandy in 1944 he was glad not to have subjected a horse to the hazards of war. And I, for one, am glad to see them no nearer danger than that in the hunting field. Didn't Surtees' Mr. Jorrocks have a final word:

"unting is all that's worth living for — all time is lost wot is not spent 'unting — it is like the hair we breathe — if we have it not we die — it's the Sport of Kings, the image of war without its guilt, and only five and twenty per cent of its danger.'

But I digress. As I dismounted *John* (incidentally a troop horse, a very good hunter which I hired from the army for 15 shillings per month, what we commonly called fifteen bobbers) I noticed that Peat was murmuring to the chestnut colt, rubbing his nose — they were already pals. Dear Peat, he was a wizard with horses.

As he took *John* off me he said, 'Well Sir, what are we going to call him?' That was typical of Peat and indeed of all my soldier grooms. They shared the horses. Whether at polo, racing, it was always we, never I.

While *John* was being unsaddled and rubbed down I gazed at this new horse, I knew with his breeding he could be a winner. There was an indefinable something about him, something which excited me and made me long to see into the times ahead. Then the Orderly Trumpeter sounded — the officers' warning to Dress for Mess.

Suddenly it came to me: 'Look at those spots Peat, I'm certain he'll do the lot and with those hocks he'll jump like a cat!' As I ran off I called back, 'That's it, *Leopard* it shall be!'

I ran, for I wanted a bath and it was a crime to be late for Mess. Fortunately we wore the old mess dress of green overalls, a green velvet waistcoat buttoned up to the neck and a short scarlet monkey jacket. Hence, in a hurry, one could simply forgo shirt, vest, pants, the lot. Just as well, for this barrack boasted only one bath to five officers.

I was there in time. My brother officers were enjoying their glass of sherry and although I seldom drank in those days, that night I helped myself to some, and then moved over to Adam. 'Thank you' I murmured, 'He's now called *Leopard,* and I know you've given me a winner.'

We drank to the great cat, to *Leopard,* so thin, so noble, so withdrawn and who yet had everything. Now, it was up to me to train him, Peat would see he was no longer half starved.

CHAPTER 2
First Steps

At York a soldier's year divided into three distinct blocks
followed by a leave period. The early months were devoted
to individual training — that involved mastery of such
things as sword drill, musketry, map reading and so on —
but for our 'green' ones, horses and men alike, right round
the year it meant slow incessant methodical training.

Those were the days when the position of the élite, the
equitation staff, the rigours and the glory that position
entailed, could hardly be questioned. The instructors of the
Cadre Noir, that magnificent French Cavalry School at
Saumur were such an élite. They still are. The same applied
to the Inniskillings as in all our cavalry regiments. My staff
was comprised of Rough Riding Sergeant Major Gough, two
Sergeants, three or four Corporals and ten remount riders
(Rough Riding incidentally one of the wilder misnomers, for
what rough rider could train a horse?). We had to train 40
to 50 young recruits and at least the same number of
untrained horses, like *Leopard*. But, I'd already decided
that *Leopard* would be trained by me alone.

Reveille pierced the dark and the wet of a typical early
Midwinter morning. Horses began to neigh and stamp,
knowing well their breakfast was only half an hour away.
Punctually to my stable for that small feed came Peat,
Turnbull and Luxford. They saddled up *Pilot*, I used him to

15

teach the first ride of recruits at half past seven. *Pilot,* with
the star on his forehead which glimmered through the dusky
morning before lights were switched on. It was always a
picture: first the horses were watered at the squadron
troughs, then as the Troop Sergeant came in with fodder,
the line of horses, expectant, did an eyes right, ears pricked
as smart as any guards drilling. Then they were mucked out
— on fine days the straw taken out into the sun but now
stacked in the centre of the stable. The Troop Sergeant had
been up to his usual tricks, hurrying about between the tins
placed behind each horse, whipping away a handful of corn
from one to give to some particular thin horse he was
cossetting.

That was the first. At midday the Squadron Trumpeter
would again sound 'To Water the Horses':

'Water your horses! Water your horses!
Water your horses — give 'em a drink!
As you know
What it is to be dry in this show,
Just give 'em a good long drink.'

Soon followed by; 'Feed'

'Feed your horses, feed your horses!
Give 'em the oats and corn!
See their ears wag!
Shows they know the "Feed" my boys,
As well as you know you're born.
Give 'em the oats and corn!'

At which one or two would paw the ground and another
might deliver his impatient snort.

Four feeds a day was the usual practice. But not in my
stable: Trooper Peat knew better. He gave smaller amounts
five or even six times a day, mindful of a horse's
comparatively small stomach.

Sharp at half past seven I arrived. *Pilot* was led out with a
plain saddle — for I'd be taking that recruit ride. As I
mounted I told Turnbull to be sure and give *Fish* his second
feed a bit early as he must have him at Sheriff Hutton by
quarter past eleven — the Middleton Meet today! 'Get him
away by nine fifteen, it's ten miles, so that you can jog along

16

at an easy five miles an hour.'

The Riding School fairly quivered with industry. Gough had given the recruit ride that familiar 'Quit your stirrups, cross stirrups, trot!' Nothing's more calculated to increase the desire for breakfast. The recruits all wore puttees, with the élite instructors easily distinguishable by their black jackboots.

Everything in order, I told Sergeant Major Gough that I would take *Leopard* out on the lunge rein, then go hunting and would be back about five and might see him in the evening. There were no 'hours'. Men worked endlessly, quite

"*I would take Leopard out on the lunge rein.*"

2.

willing because they were interested, and when something special had to be done we always rode in the evening between 6 and 9. We could concentrate then, without interruption.

After breakfast on that first memorable training day, I collected *Leopard,* ready with a cavesson head collar and long rein attached to the centre ring of the steel, leather-covered, noseband. No saddle, I'd only let him see the barracks and get to know me. Walking round the square I first led him on one side and then the other. We stopped and watched the recruits marching and drilling. When they came to the sword drill *Leopard's* ears pricked. I knew what he thought. A lunge to the right as if at a mounted opponent

17

then a lunge to the left at an infantry rifleman lying on the ground.

A little later we sauntered, that is the word, down the back, past the riding school to the rather small, indifferent training ground, a flat, well-used stretch of about ten acres known as the Low Moor. Along one side ran a lane of obstacles, about 80 yards of assorted fences, some brush, some poles, even a bank. Here the recruits learned to jump and the remounts had their first lesson loose. Personally I had no faith in these loose lanes, they encouraged young horses to rush headlong to get to the end where a Trooper waited with a tin of oats for a reward.

Leopard moved his head a little, definitely interested, quite calm as we steadily walked on together. But time was getting on too — and I must be off to change my coat and get to the Meet so, promenade over, quickly back to the stables.

'Well boy, how'd y'go, seen everything?' enquired his pal Peat.

'Fine,' I gave his guardian the rein, 'I think I'll be back early and might take him to see the school after tea.'

I hurried off to slip on a white hunting tie, or as some call it, a stock. I always seemed in a hurry. So much had to be crammed in. But who minds if you're doing what you want to do?

When I arrived with two others in my old Rover 8, Turnbull very smart in khaki, was waiting with *Flying Fish*. Oddly, it was almost as though *Leopard* had cast a spell and decided it was his day for there seemed little scent. At about three o'clock I and the other two decided to call it off.

Only five miles to jog home and as we passed the Guard Room the trumpeter sounded across the square, calling to Evening Stables:

'Up with the hay and litter down, boys?
Up with the hay and litter down, boys!
Soon as the officer's been around, boys,
Then we can go to town!'

Soon enough all horses were bedded down and fed for the night. Or rather, all but one. I believed in taking a young

18

horse out as often as possible, as a swain with his maid. As the Americans say, the sooner we get acquainted the better!

A quick tea then Peat, *Leopard* and I were off to the indoor school. This time Peat carried a saddle for I'd yet to learn whether *Leopard* had ever been ridden, or, as we call it, backed. In England there was only occasionally any worry for many of the remounts came from Ireland — very different in India where our Australian horses, known as Whalers, bucked enough to qualify for any rodeo. As we entered, Gough and one or two of the remount staff were schooling young horses — possibly those of young officers. For this they got a bit extra to supplement their meagre pay. The others wearing thick leather gloves were packing fences using gorse. Not the most enviable of tasks.

So the moment of initiation had come. In that lighted school Peat carefully approached *Leopard* with the saddle. One of the riders gave a hand, patting him quietly on the far side. With no fuss the saddle was on, the girth tightened up but not too tight. No worry. Dave had obviously ridden *Leopard,* with or without a saddle. I then mounted and had a gentle walk round. I then dismounted and passed the lunge rein to Peat. *Leopard* was never ridden by anyone but myself. One of the great advantages of lungeing is that when away, others can do it for you.

Otherwise it was a typical day. Late that evening after mess, I went out to have a look at *Fish* after his day's hunting. All were rugged up, quietly munching their hay. As I switched off the lights I heard the trumpet sound the familiar — and grateful — *'Lights Out. Lights Out . . .'*

CHAPTER 3
Initiation

We started this story with the words 'once upon a time' for only thus could I indicate certain fairy tale elements in our lives then. A cavalry regiment returning from overseas had a large number of young soldiers and young horses to train and be ready for war. It was already 1929, the most destructive war in history a mere 10 years off (or we could say exactly midway between the two most appalling wars in all history). Yet in that very year a new edition of the Manual of Cavalry Training of 1920 was published. There the General Staff, while admitting the existence of many means of conveyance more rapid than the horse, asserted that none of these could completely replace it in war, laying stress on mobility as the pre-eminent characteristic of cavalry.

However, in fact some concession had already been made to mechanisation. In 1928 the two unamalgamated junior cavalry regiments, the 12th Lancers and the 11th Hussars, had begun to exchange their horses for armoured cars, and the following year motor transport for the carriage of machine guns, minor baggage, forage, etc., previously carried on the troopers' saddles was granted to all cavalry regiments. These were the good things of life, yet the paradox is, and I must stress this, when we were finally mechanised and war came, it was above all what we'd learned with our horses which stood us in such good stead.

But that was in the ghastly future; calm, productive, enjoyable years remained to us, or to some of us, so let's return to Trooper Peat as he stands in Mr. Ansell's stable one day surveying the four polo ponies. They're still in the 'rough' though looking well, and they must gradually be got fit for the start of polo in April. Nearby the two chargers, *Pilot* and *Flying Fish*; the two indispensable 'fifteen bobbers' *Sunbeam* and *John* and the slightly aloof newcomer, *C 29*, a total of nine. This was my kingdom and, in the regiment, a kingdom within a kingdom.

York, though a domain of pleasure for the young soldier returned from outposts of the Empire, was not, apart from the hunting, an ideal place for the horse. Obvious attractions for his rider were gay shop windows, cheerful pubs, friendly people, and the products of Messrs. Terry and Rowntree could hardly fail to tempt the troops. Superb hunting with the Middleton, the York and Ainsty, the Bramham Moor, and, of course, the East Middleton where *Leopard's* sire *Maître Corbeau* had stood at stud: but training facilities — it lacked everything. The alternatives were the Low Moor, always wet and soggy, or a march through the slippery streets of the town to the Knavesmire, a larger tract of grass within the racecourse. The annual four weeks' manoeuvres had to be held at Catterick, 45 miles away. So an awful lot depended on the hunting in that ideal country, fences perhaps on the small side which permitted the 'fifteen bobber' to compete with the best provided he was well trained and ridden.

Leopard, of course, in this first year of his training was very much on the sidelines. When, early in March, his next door neighbours *Pilot* and *Flying Fish* stopped hunting, he would look sideways a little enviously when Peat took them off each day to the Knavesmire, this their period of concentrated preparation for the forthcoming point-to-points. Pupil *Leopard,* always ridden by me, would meanwhile watch the recruits or remounts, sometimes sporting a plain hunting saddle, sometimes a trooper's saddle with high arch back and front, on his near side a sword, on the right a rifle bucket, for every troop horse must learn to carry a sword and rifle.

Spring so soon becomes Summer and then the agricultural shows and fêtes were eager to engage some sort of display to vary the usual programme of hunter, pony and show jumping classes. For something spectacular they naturally looked to a Cavalry Regiment. That is how the Inniskillings came to provide a superb Musical Ride. The ordinary Cavalry Ride consisted of figures, wheeling and interlacing movements with great accuracy and smoothness — as when we danced the 'Lancers' — but in the display which began to evolve early in 1929 there was much more than this. Imagine a 'grid' of six bush fences laid out each side of the arena, in the centre two broad tables with a gap between them. Thirty horses then ridden very fast over these jumps in varying formations and directions. In a final figure the whole Ride galloped single file down the centre of the arena and jumped from table to table over a bush fence, on the flanks of which machine-guns were firing blanks. The whole display in full dress uniform, scarlet tunics, green breeches, white gauntlets, sword belt and sling and brass helmets with plumes flying — to the swirl of the Regimental Band. Each man, drawn sword carried at the slope, joined to his horse over one hundred and twenty jumps in the half-hour performance. It took four months of steady work to school horses and men to the necessary fitness and standard of performance. The men looked proud in their uniform, they loved being in full dress — and who can say the horses did not feel that too?

How popular the Searchlight Tattoos were in the twenties and thirties — if the weather was fine you could rely on huge crowds nightly, all but the cynical beguiled by that mixture of old-fashioned drill, modern physical training, marching and counter-marching of massed regimental bands, battle scenes and so on. I like to think that the highlight of our own Tattoo was hardly the least striking, mounted troops led into the arena by a trumpeter riding *Fritz,* the grey pony captured by the 5th Dragoon Guards in their charge at Harbonnières in 1918. The dash and glitter of horses and guns, the tossing heads and thundering hooves never failed to arouse the spectators. From the first moment lights blazed upon brass helmets and flashing sword blades till they blacked out just as the last horse soared between crackling machine-guns and galloped off — one continuous thunder of applause.

The Musical Ride was much sought after, but even in those days it was expensive to organise and maintain: at least thirty Troopers and their horses to be paid and a band engaged. Men weren't paid directly, of course, the money went into the funds of the Corporals' Mess, etc. That certainly helped our regiment's finances but many shows demanded a less expensive affair and so — enter the Trick Ride!

This was an instantaneous success from its opening performance at the 1929 York Polo Tournament. At first consisting of trick tent pegging, vaulting, jumping over varied and unusual obstacles, all set off by some admirable clowning. It rapidly developed in skill and daring to become what was probably the finest display of military horsemanship and showmanship produced by any regiment or anyone else.

These activities had real military value and everyone connected with them, down to the youngest fatigue man, was imbued with pride, enthusiasm and self-respect. Are those virtues really old fashioned? People who make common cause, that's the phrase that comes to mind, and the fact that the threat of being thrown out of the show was quite enough disciplinary edge. It seldom had to be used.

Does this digression take us too far from *Leopard*? I don't think so, for what he absorbed and observed in those early months was crucial to him. Who knows what *Pilot* and *Flying Fish* told him in the evenings or that he was unprepared when I arrived one day and said:

'Tomorrow I shall want *Leopard* in a troop saddle, he must learn the feel of the sword and rifle bucket.'

Next morning at seven *Leopard* eyed me inquisitively as he was led out with my sword on the near side, a rifle bucket strapped on the right or off-side. Peat had brought his rifle.

24

'Peat, give me your rifle and stand by his head.'

Taking up the reins in my left hand and transferring the rifle to the same, holding it by the muzzle, I swung my leg over the saddle and then the rifle over *Leopard's* shoulder with my right hand, into the bucket in what was really one long spiral movement. *Leopard* didn't budge an inch, he hadn't watched the recruits doing this for nothing. I drew my sword, made various passes around his head, he remained impassive. So far so good — it is so vital to have each rung strong and secure in the training ladder, particularly the bottom rungs!

I don't know if *Leopard* was envious of his stable companions in those early days. I always used *Pilot* for training the Trick Ride: he would do whatever asked but the Ride was amateurish compared with what it was to become and as yet I had no conception of what might be asked. He was also superb out hunting, when he showed how he'd earned his name. I like to think that he told *Leopard* a thing or two over the evening feed.

Leopard first came into his own when he drilled to the trumpet in squadron formation on the Knavesmire. But to get there we had that precarious ride through the centre of York at first light. Always it seemed down slippery streets, the gas lamps still dimly shining. I would look into the shop windows and get a pretty clear idea of what we looked like for on these occasions *Leopard* wore his officers' embellishments: sparkling brasses on the head dress, equally sparkling stirrup bosses with regimental crest, a white plume below his throat.

One of these days, and he was still a remount, he saw hounds for the first time when the York and Ainsty passed right in front of the Squadron. They were only on hound exercise, the hunt servants wearing grey bowlers with their red coats. Our Squadron Leader's Trumpeter sounded the 'Halt', *Leopard* pricked his ears, had a good look and silently hailed future companions.

At the end of about a year remounts and recruits had to 'pass out'. A big day, the Colonel accompanied by the Adjutant and Squadron Leaders attended the parade, a

3. *"He saw hounds for the first time, the York and Ainsty passed right in front of the Squadron."*

good deal of tension could be felt in the air. First a close inspection as to turnout, then the examination: could this young Trooper ride in exacting circumstances, use his sword well, above all take care of his horse?

Move off, Walk, Trot, Canter, Halt, Draw Swords. Our candidate would move into action, first attacking a mounted dummy, then a stuffed sack in lieu of a prone infantryman. Finally, proof that he could jump with and without stirrups. If and when the C.O. said, 'Well done,' a proud Instructor commanded his protégé, 'Carry swords', in salute to his Commanding Officer as they rode off, his troop horses impatiently tossing their heads.

In turn *Leopard* was one of those. Dare I say his white plume waved that much more fiercely, that much more freely?

I remember the day clearly, perfectly turned out, buckles and brasses shining, his imperturbable air as Trooper Peat gave him a parting pat on the neck: 'Don't you fail, you can come back here as a fifteen bobber even, but not as a remount.'

I hope *Leopard* wasn't peeked by it, as I'd trained him he

couldn't compete for the coveted prize awarded to the best remount rider.

The Trick Ride and Musical Ride were in full swing and although responsible for both I only rode in the first; for that I relied on *Pilot*.

Summer now, and I rode either *Flying Fish* or *Leopard* when instructing or leading my troop on parade, as we approached the climax of the year. All but a few were ordered to Catterick about 45 miles away for Regimental Training, and although my new horse was only five years old Peat agreed that I should take him, for the experience, with *Flying Fish*. The rest stayed behind to enjoy a well-earned rest.

Bright one morning, in August, the Regiment paraded before setting off on the march to Catterick. We would do the 45 miles in the day, averaging 5 miles an hour, and although lorries now transported a good deal of our stuff

"Each trooper was a sort of mounted hive."

4.

each horse was carrying about 19 stone. Each trooper was a sort of mounted hive with sword, rifle, bandolier, nose-bag, water bucket, his haversack on the left side with a mug hooked through the strap, water bottle on the right, ground sheet strapped across the front arch of his saddle and that oh, so, resplendently burnished mess tin clipped to the rifle bucket. An officer had no haversack but wallets on either side of the saddle in front of his knees. Every horse carried a spare set of shoes and if no farrier was available the Troop Officer had been trained to put them on.

The commanding officer, Lt. Col. R. Evans' Trumpeter sounded the 'mount' and then the 'walk march' and the C.O. set off followed by him and an Orderly carrying a lance with his flag aloft, red, yellow and green, the Regimental Crest embroidered. Each Squadron Leader would follow suit giving identical orders. Even in those days a regiment would have stopped all traffic had it not allowed intervals between Squadrons and Troops: in half section, two abreast, a Troop covered some 60 yards and a Regiment of four Squadrons would probably have stretched well over a mile. Therefore a distance of 20-30 yards between troops, 50 between Squadrons, was the rule.

5. *". . . and an Orderly carrying a lance."*

6. ". . . in half sections, two abreast, a Troop covered some 60 yards."

As we moved through the then traffic-free streets of York, *Leopard* and I checked up on our appearance in the shop windows. I certainly seemed to be sitting up smartly and straight, and *Leopard*, kept his head in the correct position with a touch of disdain, and walked with long strides to keep that white plume flowing under his throat.

Once out of the town the Colonel's Trumpeter sounded the Regimental call followed by 'The Trot' and before long came the 'March at Ease' quickly repeated by Squadron Trumpeters all down the line. Ease and bliss, for the Troopers could now talk and smoke, but pipes only. Yet few smoked, I certainly never did. Trotting along we could gaze down over the hedges into front gardens and have a good look into every car — many were open then. What sort of a chap was that driving? On a job? His attractive wife, or was it a lady friend . . .? *Leopard* couldn't work up any interest in mere motor cars but he turned a critical eye on those young horses galloping round a field. He thought 'they think they're lucky but how can they compare with me? I who am trained and with my white plume, I'm a very proud horse.'

By about noon we were nearly half way to Catterick and

halted for possibly two hours. A field was at our disposal and here the cooks (who had gone ahead in the lorries) had prepared a hot stew for the men, and canvas water troughs for the horses had been erected and filled from a nearby stream. What a change from India, with those small Army Transport carts pulled, or hardly pulled, by reluctant mules!

First the horses would be off-saddled, backs rubbed and smacked, the bits removed and then they were watered and their feed brought to them in the nose-bags. Only after that would the men fetch their still shining mess tins and while one stayed with a pair of horses the other would draw a couple of tins of stew. But a man wouldn't dream of feeding himself until his horse had that white nose-bag on.

So to Catterick. This new life, the second new life within a year, was a bit of a surprise for *Leopard*. But he didn't worry, he trusted Peat and *Flying Fish* kept up his morale. Yet could here be his new stable on the side of this hill, the ground bright with heather in full flower, and down the near side and that side, lines of bell tents? In the centre of a square, long lengths of rope about 5 feet from the ground, every 6 feet or so a peg driven in with a length of rope and a shackle attached.

A little bemused, *Leopard* barely heard Peat's quiet 'Come on, old boy', the while being shackled to his off hind fetlock. Quite comfortable though, and easy to lie down in this deep, deep heather. Anyway, *Fish* would advise him. *Fish* knew about these things.

Now saddles had been set down behind each horse. What grander sight could anyone wish to see than over 300 horses in line after line? Rapidly each man rubbed down his horse and dried him off. All sweat marks gone. It certainly had been hot this lovely August day. When the order was given to water, Peat led *Leopard* and his companion to have a good drink saying, 'Go on then, I must get you watered and fed then I'll be off for my pint or maybe two.'

Back at the lines, tied and shackled, rugs on, our two horses like the others were ready for a feed, which Peat drew from that old soldier Trooper Knott into a nosebag. Nosebags on, neighs of delight, now the tired Troopers could take saddles, swords and rifles to their bell tents. Horses fed now they could have a meal, a fine hot one too.

But the day's work is not yet done. When the call rings out to *'Hay up'* Peat ties a net full of hay to the line. *Leopard* and *Flying Fish* will be happy for the night.

So at last, 'Fall Out' and the Main Guard and Stable Guard take over, smart as always even after the long ride. Peat and his pals sink that long draught of a pint and more in the canteen. Who among us could have guessed how this 'holiday camp' would end that August? Augusts have a habit of surprises.

Reveille sounded next morning and all was bustle and activity although a day of so-called rest. Horses have to be groomed as relentlessly. Shoes looked at, the Troop Farrier waiting in his outdoor forge. Then the Troopers settled down in the sun to clean saddles and bridles, to polish those swords and 'pull through' their rifles with that bit of flannel known as a four by two. Everything must be ready for the start of training next day.

The second evening the men went off to see what joys Catterick had to offer. Not many I fear. Returning late, as the Night Guard with their lanterns quietly walked around they sought out their sleeping quarters. A Section, or eight men, slept in each of these bell tents. Rifles and swords fastened to the centre pole, the men slept outwards with their feet against them. Such was the precaution learnt on the North West Frontier of India.

CHAPTER 4
Baptism of Fire

How glorious the weather and although the actual training area on Catterick moorland was restricted it was beautiful to ride over, undulating and nearly knee deep in heather. *Leopard* enjoyed this too, only occasionally startled when a covey of grouse rose suddenly. But the area was too small and consequently all our battles, however ingeniously designed, whether with or against the two Infantry Brigades, always seemed to finish on a lofty hill. Every battle ended on Barden Fell.

Early in the morning when Peat had saddled *Leopard*, C Squadron would move off to some distant village, ten or fifteen miles away. Here my Squadron Leader, 'How' Wiley, would receive his orders, orders fresh with surprise. Once again 'Reconnoitre Barden Fell' or 'Attack Barden Fell'. If the former our orders were simple; 'Mike, we're to reconnoitre Barden Fell and find out if held by enemy troops. It's possible that it may be held and quickly reinforced, so we must get there first. Today, you'll be the leading Troop, we move off at 0900 hours, move quickly and remember, first avoid any umpires and then the enemy.' *Leopard* took in the bit about moving quickly.

Back with my Troop I had a brief look at the map and we were off for Barden Fell, the leading section headed by a young would-be officer called John Anderson (later General

Sir John Anderson). At that time he was still at Oxford, a scholar from Winchester, and what he must have thought is not so difficult to imagine but the orders were simple: 'Go like hell, Barden Fell. We must get there first. Keep clear of all umpires and if you meet one don't stop.'

Leopard soon realised there was no stopping on our way to Barden Fell, up and down the lanes and then into the deep heather on the moor. On, on, on, on — a short skirmish with some infantry but we needn't count that, not an umpire in sight. We covered some fifteen miles in well under two hours and at Barden Fell my troop took up positions of defence, *Leopard* was led away with others, three men in four dismounting, their rifles fully charged. Finally the attack from the infantry until the Trumpet sounded *'Cease Fire'* followed by the inevitable call, *'All officers come and be damned, all officers come and be damned'*.

My Troop Sergeant 'Hoot' Jones took over then and *Leopard* was brought up looking a shade wistful, he knew his pals would be watered at any stream and fed before returning to camp but he might have to wait.

The time went by in eternal sunshine, sometimes we worked through the day, at others during the night. How wonderful it was to be free, away from traffic, the Low Moor and York. But heat can rarely stay constant. When it becomes intense something must break, must go. We had returned from a long tactical exercise late in the evening. The horses had just been watered and fed when the low sky seemed to heave over, slowly turning a curious coffee colour. The air was so thick we could barely breathe until — a crash of thunder, when the sky seemed to jump apart in halves as a snake of orange fire slashed through to hit the earth in the centre of our camp. Rain, torrents of it, as the Orderly Trumpeter sounded the alarm:

'Larm is sounding what's up now?
Fire or fight or jolly row?
Into togs and off we go!'

No time for togs. Everyone was running from the tents to the horses, officers shouting, 'Stand to your horses.' No one panicked as thunder roared again, twice and three times. Another flash of lightning. The rain was suddenly stinging hail. Horses were rearing and kicking, heel shackles gone in the mud which moments before had been a field. Peat had reached *Leopard* and *Fish,* 'Steady now, steady, we'll be all right. I'm with you now, keep quiet' as he rubbed my *Leopard's* ears and muzzle. *Fish,* an old campaigner, knew he needn't worry with Peat nearby.

Yet another livid flash, third time into our lines, and several Troopers fell with their charges, one killed as were both the horses he held. That storm roared on for an hour or more while the men stood soaked to the skin quietly patting and calming their terrified horses. No panic, no stampede, just a gentle pat on the horse's neck and, 'Now boy, don't get worried, what about me?'

Then the sky lightened a little and we could see the camp. That deep black mud, had it been gay heather? The drenched men still standing with their horses. Not one had broken away.

"The rain never stopped."

7.

Everything ends, the clouds eventually lifted. The Divisional General was there to see what could be done. Dry rugs, dry blankets and underclothes, extra men to help raise the flattened tents. And rum, a double rum ration, a feed for the horses and soon the men were singing in that black mud. All but one.

It was the end of our manoeuvres; the rain never stopped. The order came to return to York. Making fine time at 6 miles an hour we rode proudly into Fulford Barracks soon after four. The Regiment formed up on the bleak tarmac square and the order echoed around us: 'Prepare to dismount, dismount!' Each man stood by his horse and waited for the C.O.'s Trumpeter to sound the 'Dismiss':

'This is the Call we like?
It makes you feel all right —
There's no call comes up to "No Parade"!'

At my stable Luxford took *Fish* and Turnbull led in *Leopard,* Peat following with the comforting words, "Well, lad, you've been christened the hard way!'

CHAPTER 5
Now Hunting

Drama can be exhilarating, it tautens the nerves, tunes us to act beyond our normal capacity. Nevertheless *Leopard* and *Flying Fish* were more than a little grateful to be led in that evening, while Turnbull and Luxford, quick to see how tired Peat looked, took over with their usual competence. But although he was exhausted *Leopard* noticed there were two newcomers to the stable and thought, 'I must ask *Pilot* what's been happening.'

A bright young chestnut, *King Edgar*, shook and lifted his head to give *Leopard* a bit of a glare: He's rather good looking' observed *Leopard,* only to overhear Peat muttering nearby, 'There's something not too sure about that one' — as though he'd sensed what *Leopard* was thinking! Sure enough, worn out as he was Peat had wanted to check up on each of his protégés. True, I had bought *King Edgar* for a mere £20 but he show-jumped well and later even qualified for the Royal Tournament. Then, almost as though his shining coat couldn't contain his fire, he broke blood vessels. These tragedies are only too common.

Leopard pondered before going to sleep, as he always did when anything struck him. He reckoned he knew quite a lot about hunting — hadn't I taken him out some afternoons with my two daschshunds, *Freddy* and his winsome wife *Freda,* past that ridiculous training area, the Low Moor and on to Escrick Common? Why in Germany they're badger hounds and that's hunting, isn't it? They now had five offspring which brought the Escrick Common pack up to strength with a total of seven! That bare bit of common land was so pockmarked you could hardly take a step without treading in a rabbit hole, yet though *Freddy* and his *Family Pack* hunted boldly and with a good cry, somehow they never seemed to catch a rabbit. But what could this hunting be that *Pilot* and *Flying Fish* conferred so earnestly about? Surely not rabbiting? Musing thus *Leopard* faded first into a doze and soon down to a deep sleep.

The Master of the Middleton Hounds was Colonel 'Peach' Borwick. I felt a certain anxiety when asking him if I might bring out some of my recruits and young horses to the cub hunting meets in October. This would be my chance to initiate *Leopard*. Of course the late Chief Instructor of the Cavalry School and the Colonel of the Scots Greys replied: 'Certainly, go ahead!'

Of the three hunting areas within easy reach of York, Sheriff Hutton, Sand Hutton and Strensall, the last place was no place for a young horse — small deep ditches hidden by grass caused endless tumbles — and the big jumps, the first could be disastrous for beginners. Sand Hutton then opened *Leopard's* new chapter of experience.

An early start is essential for cub hunting. Around five o'clock, Peat, the remount riders and I were awake. Our horses had an early feed. Before even the Night Guard came off duty we'd slipped away through the dimmed streets of York towards Aldby — our host Colonel Borwick thrilled to see us there — thence we moved off to Buttercrambe Moor. *Leopard* shivered at the sight of these hounds. What were we going to do now? The young remount riders equally expectant and is that surprising? Monotony is the hell of all life. Variety is more than the spice of life, it's the very essence. What price this after life in Barracks? On Buttercrambe Moor we soon heard hounds 'speaking ' — a fox — and quickly ran to Sand Hutton, another large wood, on the way a few fences to be jumped. Superlative training this for the young rider, young horse, for the cavalryman who within ten years would successfully command a tank or

38

armoured car. Knowledge is power. Each commander had to choose his own line.

We finished that morning as so often, near Whitesike Farm: a steaming cup of tea, and we said thank you to the Master and his splendid kennel huntsman, Stanley Barker. We rode off, happy.

Such was our life during the leave season, two-thirds of the men away while recruits and remounts continued training. How could I complain of that, of almost unlimited hunting?

I was determined *Leopard* should not have a day's real hunting until 6 years old, in January, for all horses count their years from that month. We cannot count the cub hunting and his entry into manhood, so to speak, took place at the Askham Grange Meet on a Tuesday. The best of the York and Ainsty country was nearly all grass where the generous Master, David Lycett-Green, had reinforced many of the fences with perfect posts and rails.

Sharp at half past nine *Leopard* was led out. He turned his head ever so slightly as I mounted, that red coat would become a familiar sight to him. As we passed through the Main Gate the sentry saluted smartly by 'Carrying Sword', I acknowledged by slightly lifting my top hat. York's citizens are used to seeing those off hunting and over Skeldergate Bridge we went and out on the Tadcaster Road. Passing the York racecourse and the Knavesmire in the distance we saw a train coming up from Leeds: the smoke billowed and hung low — sure sign of a good scenting or hunting day. '*Leopard*,' I breathed, 'you're going to bring me luck on your first hunt. Don't forget what I've taught you'. Past Buckles Inn we turned right and were soon in the park, and there in front of the large red house sat mounted Charlie Littleworth, the huntsman, surrounded by some twenty couple of hounds. The bitch pack; so if all went well we were in for a good day. A round of greetings with an air of subdued cheerfulness peculiar to meets, good morning to the Master, a quick word with Charlie the Huntsman and Matt Snell, the first whipper-in.

The first draw would be Harewood Whin, I'd guessed.

Leopard and I moved in the direction hounds would take. Then I hopped off and had a good look at his shoes, all the clinches down and so they should be, though, incidentally, we only paid five shillings a set of shoes, then I checked his girths and remounted. Charlie gave a touch on his horn and we were moving off.

'Now *Leopard* my lad, I repeat no mistakes today and remember all we've learned together.'

Sure enough the draw was Harewood Whin, about sixty of us out. *Leopard* and I slipped in behind the Master. Half-a-crown in the 'cap' on the way for the wire fund, not that there was any wire to be pulled down in this superb Tuesday country.

Arrived at the covert our Master took his stand beside a gate, the field closing in on him with much chatter and excited laughter. I decided that as this was to be *Leopard's* baptism we would go on our own — and there, under a tree, I saw a nice post and rails. He was used to rails and we could always see what was on the other side. We listened. A hound spoke, then another, *Leopard* pricked his ears. Now a holloa from Matt as our fox left the top end of the Whin. I looked over to our Master who began to open the gate. Always at that stage the suspense makes everything seem to move in slow motion; when we were over I softly said, 'Come on boy, now is our day.'

The fox skirted Grange Wood and over to Askham Strips, hardly a ploughed field, nearly all dairy farming. Hounds now swung to Askham Bog, a famous covert of nearly fifty acres, scrub with a few oak and silver birch. Now, after half a century, it is a nature reserve. *Leopard* was well up, for we'd been on the inside but hardly quick enough, hounds were through and streaming over the main Tadcaster-York road. That couldn't happen now. It is a motorway. *Tempus fugit,* and not, I'm afraid, time only.

We'd reached the main road. Now came my problem. Hounds were screaming away, I knew the scent was good — smoke from that train had billowed low. The field swung left, knowing the country, should we follow the field or follow hounds? Charlie and Matt I saw going ahead after hounds, but they knew the country. I knew *Leopard,* I did not know the country, but follow hounds we would. Three of us only now, over several grass fields, and here we were at the Leeds-York main railway line! A steep embankment with the usual creosoted post and rails.

Pulling back *Leopard* almost to a trot, we were over the post and rails, nothing to those on the Low Moor, up the embankment, no sign of a train, hounds all over. *Leopard* stood poised taking a good look at the signal wires, then carefully picked up his feet over these and the lines, down the other side another post and rails, and we were away. I could see Matt and the hounds but not at that time Charlie.

What bliss this was, thought *Leopard* and I. So much grass, the fields small, occasionally ploughland with a light furrow to gallop down. The Master and all the field were away on our left having crossed the rails by road and bridge.

After about a mile Charlie was back with us just as we came to our second hazard, the main London-York line. Our luck was in. Signals up and no cutting or embankment. *Leopard* now felt almost as nonchalant with signal wires and lines as with those old post and rails.

Mr. Fox had obviously been making for Knavesmire Wood but had been headed, so we rounded Bishopthorpe and found ourselves in the vegetable garden of the Archbishop of York. And here I stood with *Leopard,* holding the horses of Charlie and Matt. I'm afraid hounds had killed their fox among His Grace's brussels sprouts.

That had been quite an initiation. A four mile point, about seven as hounds ran, two railway lines to cross. *Leopard* was 'with the angels', as the French say.

As we peacefully made our way home I knew his three protectors, Peat, Turnbull and Luxford would be in the stable to greet him. A good mash and what stories to tell! Would *Pilot* or *Flying Fish* believe him? *Leopard* didn't care very much about that, for he'd enjoyed himself. This was only a beginning.

CHAPTER 6
The Spice of Life

Monotony is hell. I have said that already. I'll say it again. Those familiar with military life, and many who aren't, often assert that tedium is unavoidable — that the repetition of drill and training must make for sameness. I dispute that. Certainly in my Regiment, before the war, we went to considerable lengths in search of variety. System is one thing, uniformity another.

Our recruits, for example, would sometimes be given the choice of either going off to a meet of the hounds as a 'ride' or finding their way individually, by different routes, to improve their map-reading. Again, on Sunday after Church Parade, remount riders who'd been out with a young horse would be quite happy to pile into a 15 cwt. truck, armed with bill hooks, hammers and spades to help the farmers mend fences. After all, it was a day in the country away from barracks and a pint or two of ale from a grateful farmer not to be sniffed at. I cannot see that being allowed today.

I'm merely lifting a corner of the curtain to show the scene in which *Leopard* grew up. The curtain came down and stayed down in 1939.

Leopard was by now fully trained. But we never knew what might happen from day to day. Calamity is always just round the corner. Sure enough, he was hauled out of his apprenticeship to assume his full responsibilities sooner than he expected. Early in March fate struck. One day, while hunting near Sheriff Hutton on *Pilot,* the field turned left but I followed hounds. Coming to a fence which looked nothing, innocently concealing a nearly unjumpable ditch beyond, *Pilot's* forelegs landed on the bank, hind legs in the ditch. When I'd helped him out I saw how desperately lame he was and led him the 9 miles back to York. Peat did all the usual, all he could, hot compresses to his shoulder, a good feed of mash of linseed and bran. He was terribly lame and poor *Pilot* thought his name a little inappropriate that night, and realised his friend *Leopard* would have to take over.

Fortunately for *Leopard,* he'd spent many an hour muzzling with *Pilot,* ensuring that now, like any good soldier, he would be ready to take on. For among the others, although *Flying Fish* was older, he hadn't the calm temperament. As for those polo ponies, they had an easy life, cossetted until their season of only five months in the year. At six years old *Leopard* must now hunt, demonstrate to recruits, perform in the Trick Ride, exhibit the use of the sword, and carry himself with an air when pioudly dressed for ceremonial parades. Fortunately, he had taken over more and more from *Pilot,* while the latter never recovered from the injury to his shoulder but consoled himself grazing in Aldby Park under the eye of Colonel 'Peach' Borwick.

Our regimental Trick Ride had now entered its second year. Though still a very amateur production it was inevitably much in demand, for the travelling costs were small compared with those of the full Musical Ride and Band (that involved 60 men and 35 horses besides the props). We were a dedicated group in the Trick Ride. Each evening we assembled in the Riding School to bring our venture a step nearer perfection. Trick tent pegging featured prominently in the programme. A rider would bear down and lance a peg that might be flaming with rags soaked in paraffin, or it could be attached to the clown's skirt which, when whipped away, would 'leave Corporal Samuels roaring in a rather old-fashioned pair of bloomers. All were experts with the lance, Gough and Sergeant

Hodgson being Champion Men-at-Arms of India and England respectively. The vaulters were led by Sergeant Rushton, he vaulted as dashingly as he kept goal for the 'Skins' when they won the Army Cup, the first Cavalry Regiment to do so. I remember Corporal Almond in a ballet dress topped by a platinum blonde wig! One of the clowns, Corporal Samuels, whose tumbling rôle made such a contrast with his other self, our very correct Officers' Mess Corporal. He looked more than spruce in his Blues. Those were the days when, on Guest Nights, the other Mess waiters still wore their white wigs, green tail coats, knee breeches and stockings and high striped waistcoat. This livery they kept up until the war but at some point before 1939 the wig went. Green trousers replaced knee breeches.

The second part of the ride was devoted to jumping. Now *Leopard* started to take the lead which he always held. But, I repeat, at York we were still amateurs. Various obstacles were jumped, from Sergeant Rushton on a stretcher to a fence full of fireworks, very much exploding. At Bakewell, later, we had paraffin burning the grass at least 6 feet from the fence on both sides, this by accident. But, undoubtedly we raised our standards most by the use of a bewildering assortment of narrow fences, only two or three feet wide and without wings. On one occasion, while watching at the Great Yorkshire Show, Trooper Hunting turned to a spectator and said, 'Go on, clap, isn't that fine?' — to provoke the dour Yorkshire reply, 'Surely, those horses have eyes'.

Joe Thornton, a second-hand dealer in York, was our costumier, supplying us with a most motley collection of hats (top hats, policemen's helmets, straw boaters, the well-known soft bowler). He also came to our assistance in coats — a very nice undertaker's for Sergeant Major Tennuci which, although liable to burst, only cost five bob (it was strongly rumoured that the Sergeant Major had been seen promenading down to York in it, on his way to the orchestra stalls at the Empire!) .

The Regimental Bootmaker and Tailor were similarly kept rather busy, a bit of a shock sometimes to be asked to produce a smart pair of shoes for an old short-tailed grey polo pony or trousers with the seat hanging down to his ankles for a large man like Sergeant Rushton. But, all was done willingly and with great good humour.

Leopard soon learned that life meant more than the excitement and gay freedom of the hunting field.

At that time Tattoos were staged in all the major Army centres, partly to provide funds for the Army Charities, partly to encourage young men to join the Army. York being no exception a Tattoo was held on the Knavesmire, the middle of York Race Course. The Tattoo had its origin in a simple Army routine, observed at least as far back as the 17th Century. When operations in the field ceased in the Autumn of each year, the regiments returned to take up their winter quarters in the towns and villages. Expectedly the local inns and taverns were havens for the troops, so the men must somehow be plucked from their refuges and each evening, between half past nine and ten a drummer accompanied by the Orderly Officer and a Sergeant marched through the streets beating his drum. As the drum beats echoed down the streets, inn keepers called 'Tap To' and proceeded to turn off the beer taps. 'Tap To' slurred into 'Tattoo'.

But, by our time it was no longer the drummer thundering down village streets or even a procession of massed bands: Cavalry, Royal Horse Artillery and Infantry units used the occasion to show themselves off with great lavishness and display. That is how *Leopard* came to find himself carrying me through the streets of York, the sun making a mirror of my already shining armour, himself in the full panoply of a mediaeval war horse. I led the Yorkist Army against the Lancastrians at the Battle of Bosworth Field. Alas, the Red Rose prevailed and we were defeated, though happy to witness and celebrate the nuptials of Henry VII and our beloved Elizabeth of York. If only I could have known then that another Elizabeth of York would one day, and not so very distantly, be our Queen! Each night for five nights *Leopard* and I led the Yorkist Army through York's main streets, the pennants of our lance heads fluttering, banners and standards erect. It was the most glorious play acting, all the way to the Knavesmire we were cheered by the citizens of York, followed by the Lancastrians who were being equally and naturally booed. On arrival we dismounted behind tall canvas depicting the city walls of mediaeval York. Much laughter and a little practical joking while we fed our horses and drank some beer to fortify ourselves for the fray.

The 'Stand To' sounded and we all moved off in pitch darkness to the far side of the polo ground in the middle of the Race Course. Then, on came the searchlights to reveal the opposing armies formed up on the fields of Bosworth. The trumpets blared. With lance at the ready and broadsword drawn (dummies fortunately) we charged. Dummies luckily, for each night the charge became a little more rugged and realistic. By Saturday *Leopard* and I were glad to be greeted by Peat about midnight and to remove that singularly ineffective armour!

Life in a Cavalry regiment could hardly be called humdrum for any horse. Certainly not for *Leopard*. I was thankful not to have to go to Catterick again that year for Regimental Training. Happily I remained behind in charge of the training of recruits and some more young remounts.

CHAPTER 7
A Great Day

Autumn was early that year. One evening Peat and I reviewed the coming winter. The great friend and adviser to all our stable, *Pilot,* the brown with a vivid star on his forehead, was still at Aldby, and alas, still lame. When the cold weather came of course he would return, but meanwhile we decided to put *Flying Fish* into his box. That high couraged chestnut could tell *Leopard* a thing or two, give him a different slant on things from *Pilot.*

After 'Lights Out' when they munched their hay in preparation for sleep, then was their time for weighing the pros and cons of the future — a very serious matter that — interspersed with reflections, not to say rather personal remarks about their comrades. These discussions tended to become a little heated.

Leopard quietly thought 'My day's nothing but a timetable: half past seven Recruit Instruction, half past ten, showing Remounts what they should do, half past eleven either practise or demonstrate my Dummy Thrusting, and what use is that sword going to be, I'd like to know? After my dinner I have to watch the Musical Ride rehearsing and then, to cap it all, go to the school again in the evening to practise and think out new turns for the Trick Ride. 'Trick' be damned, it's the ultimate in training and obedience and is it fair that I usually only hunt on the Fridays and never the best of the Middleton Country, and to crown everything, in Summer I'm expected to jog through York dressed up in armour, not getting back until midnight!"

Flying Fish looked down his nose, 'You have a lot to learn, you're rather young, though perhaps in time we might see you steeplechasing and possibly, but I doubt it, even doing a little show jumping.'

My *Leopard,* now thoroughly bored with the discussion thought another munch of that good hay much more sensible that a retort, and soon fell fast asleep.

Every evening, if it was not too late, I joined Sergeant Major Gough, Sergeant Hodgson and Sergeant Lee, among other Troopers in the Riding School and we devised new jumps, just as *Leopard* said. He was learning to jump anything and everything. For instance, he would walk through a jet of water from a hose if I asked him to. He, with *Gertie, Greasy* and *Red Lady* were learning how to be obedient. They were never dominated. I could never express the joy I felt.

One Saturday, the Middleton met at Leppington. The first draw at Parkers Thorns where we found and ran through Acklam about four miles from Aldby in the best of the Saturday country. We came to some large post and rails, well over 4 feet on a high bank. On the take-off side lay a ditch about 3 feet wide and 5 feet from the rails, impossible to jump the two together. Hounds were running fast. I was excited, so I left it to *Leopard* to negotiate. We jumped the ditch at an angle of 45 degrees, thus gaining more room on landing. Then from almost a trot, over the rails. The rest of the field swung left through a gate which I hadn't seen. It was only afterwards, thanks to *Leopard's* suppleness, that I realised how large this fence had been. The following Sunday I had luncheon at Aldby with Colonel 'Peach' Borwick. Late that afternoon after collecting Stanley Barker, we all examined the fence and *Leopard's* hoof marks. It was conclusive, he had the ability to jump like a cat.

Friends have asked me how I managed to train *Leopard.* I do not know! He was a horse with a superb character. We understood each other. But that understanding only came from hours together on the gradual, firm growth of a mutual trust. A trust worth more than anything when it comes to hunting.

Once a year, it was customary for the Chief Instructor at the Equitation School, Weedon, to visit each Cavalry Regiment. I was fortunate enough to have Lt. Col. Arthur Brooke as my principal instructor during my time there. He was more than knowledgeable. He was an exceptional person. Imagine my pleasure when told that he would like to come to York to see my recruits and remounts early in February. He would arrive on a Thursday evening, returning on the Sunday. He enjoyed hunting.

Naturally I determined to hunt on both the Friday and Saturday. With Peat we carefully discussed how we would mount our distinguished visitor.

Late on Thursday Arthur Brooke arrived in his small open motor car. He was a great advocate of fresh air. If you drove with him when he had a cold you were unlucky, for he believed the cure was to open everything — hood, side screens, even the windscreen. That would fix any cold.

Next morning, at seven, we awaited inspection in the school. I, savouring the thought that Peat at that moment would be getting our horses fed and away to the Pocklington Meet, 13 miles distant, arriving at noon. They'd wait for us at the local pub and then we hoped to pick up hounds. Charles Keightley, the Adjutant, would make up the party for through him would come the 'rocket' if anything looked wrong with our training.

In my diary: 7 a.m.: ride of remounts, riders more than smart, black boots shone like the moon in a lake: later to bring back thoughts of Saumur, the Cadre Noir, at the French Cavalry School.

9 a.m.: a good breakfast, then first ride of recruits, smarter than ever: typical of the British soldier, he never lets his officer down.

10.30 a.m.: second remount ride; every rider had repolished his boots. At Saumur an Orderly stands at the doors to give the last flick, a final polish before you enter the 'cathedral' of riding schools.

By quarter past eleven Arthur Brooke was satisfied and all three of us hurried to change and be off in my old car. Trooper Hunting, my soldier servant, was with us to bring it back, for without doubt we would ride home.

So far a glorious day but rather weird with a high sky, a good breeze and a few heavy clouds drifting over. Well, I'd emphasised to my Chief Instructor that Pocklington was never the best of meets, really an appetiser for what we hoped he'd have on Saturday.

The horses were at The Feathers when we arrived around one o'clock. Peat led *John* over to Colonel Arthur and gave me *Leopard*. I wish I could remember the name of Charles Keightley's horse. The evening before I had telephoned Colonel 'Peach' to give my excuses in advance and the reason why I would be late. He'd hinted that he wouldn't hurry and would be drawing towards Allerthorpe Common, not very attractive country, wild certainly, but with deep ditches — no, not ditches, dykes. The only way to cross them was to slither down one side, jump across the bottom and crawl up the other side. Towards that Common we set our course, frequently stopping to listen. No sound for about a mile and then, unmistakably the intermittent cry of hounds. All three horses became tense, as thrilled as we were. But now for our keenest ears, and we approached slowly, for were we to head the fox the Master would hardly contain his wrath — and rightly.

Thank heavens we could see hounds, running slowly over this bad scenting bit of common. The dog pack, though, and they would stick to it. The field not great for this unfashionable meet, thirty to forty at most, with many from the Inniskillings.

Suddenly, the pace began to quicken and the cry to rise, hounds now really running, the grass better and away they could go. Now we were with the field and ahead of us I saw something bigger than those dreaded dykes, hounds attempting to jump it, falling short. The field, knowing the country, bore off to the left towards a bridge half a mile away. Oh that trap of knowing your country too well, trying to be clever, when you don't follow hounds you're cheated of the prize. Arthur Brooke, Charles and I with two or three Inniskillings did follow hounds that day, for we didn't know the country.

Approaching what seemed to be a main sewer I looked for somewhere to jump it — I knew a clump of thorns would mean a sound bit of bank. Then I looked again and laughed. Our 'sewer' was the old Pocklington Canal. Well, if hounds could try to jump it we would — for they were over and streaming away. Charles went on my left, landed against the far bank where it was obviously deep, but was soon out. *Leopard* seemed to know and jumped in the middle. He didn't fall but I did, and quickly up again. Our Chief Instructor fell, I regret to say, and *John,* his horse, unfeelingly got out on the take-off side, while his rider stood wet to the skin on the opposite bank. Four or five others in similar situation, but *Leopard* and I, and Charles were clear.

The country changed, those dykes passed, and here nothing but grass in the York and Ainsty wild country, running towards the Holderness side. A few bullocks in the fields and starlings galore, but not a man to be seen. Regular as a heart beat the deep haunting cry of the dog pack as they struggled to keep on the scent. Charles fell, but I knew he had hold of his horse and on we followed. How wonderful the sky, clouds heavier now and more of them and then one would split revealing a brief glaring light.

8. "*Charles having fallen, we were alone, I talked and whispered to Leopard.*"

Charles, having fallen, we were alone and I talked and whispered to *Leopard.* The clouds, the mad, fitful light, the relentless cry of the dog hounds, green plover circling — and — wrapped round it all, that solitude, how could I ever forget it? *Leopard* felt all that too.

For three or four miles we talked together, just following until, almost as though we'd crept up on a mirage I saw hounds had come to a halt and were marking their fox to ground. I slipped off *Leopard,* loosened his girths and thanked him as he nuzzled me.

Within five minutes the field had arrived. Colonel 'Peach' and Stanley was delighted, for they loved any young soldier who enjoyed hunting and having a go. As the following day was fashionable Saturday the Master decided to call it a day. We thanked him and set off for the ride home.

After dinner I went out to say goodnight and 'thank you' again to *Leopard.* What a changed horse from that chestnut colt of 1928. Now well fed, happy and only too keen to give his best.

After a morning in the Riding School we had a satisfactory hunt in the best of the Saturday country. Lt. Col. Arthur Brooke enjoyed himself — his report was more than good.

CHAPTER 8
Skill with or without Arms

One week in March of the following year, *Leopard* became distracted by the sight of men bustling around and packing up. Peat looked a little down in the mouth. He stood by the door and expected Turnbull and Luxford to commiserate while he complained: 'Just when the horses were well settled and *Leopard* enjoying the hunting.' Turnbull hunched his shoulders and retorted, 'To hell with *Leopard* and his hunting, I've just got to know a nice lass from Terry's Chocolate Factory and now we're off to . . . Aldershot.'

Leopard had never actually been on a train though he'd looked at them once or twice at level crossings, while out hunting, and had been mildly astonished by the snorting beasts — with wheels where legs should have grown. So he watched with great interest when *Fish* and poor *Pilot,* still lame, were helped to what appeared to be a comfortable wagon at York station. Those two were used to it for on certain Saturdays they'd travelled thus to the meet of the York and Ainsty Foggathorpe country. These spacious coaches carried six horses in two lines of three facing inwards, whilst Peat, Turnbull and Luxford (or their equivalents) sat or lay on the saddlery in between. This of course being 'First Class' travelling. But the ordinary troop horse travelled second — or third class as we then called it — ten to a cattle truck, five facing one way with the other five looking in the opposite direction. If any prospective passenger felt doubtful of this accommodation two men linked friendly but strong arms behind his quarters and half lifted, half shoved, in went the reluctant traveller.

Aldershot was important as the centre of any British Expeditionary Force. From here the 5th Dragoon Guards had left in 1914 — their order to mobilise indicated by the hoisting of three black balls to a mast at Headquarters on August 3rd. They'd left with the 1st Cavalry Brigade and now the Inniskillings returned to that same 1st Brigade, together with the 7th and 8th Hussars.

Warburg Barracks were little different from those at York in *Leopard's* estimation. A good smell of cooking comforted him with the thought that, the Squadron cookhouse being next door, only a little beyond Trooper Knott would be mixing the feeds in the forage store. Once again our friend the Health Inspector would not have approved, with the barrack rooms above ensuring both men and horses were warm and comfortable.

One improvement both *Leopard* and I enjoyed, instead of York's prison-like wall we looked across the square to Wellington Avenue, soon to be lit by the candles of those fine chestnut trees. Leopard would miss his hunting, but he had a much larger training area. Anyway, what did it matter, men and horses soon learned to 'Follow the Drum' and our drums had beat the order to move to Aldershot.

The Riding School that greeted us could be called magnificent, but what a drab colour! We quickly set about repainting, the old trick of using a bright cream to give the illusion of more space. The great mirrors we'd brought from York and soon additional ones from old houses — I picked them up at auctions — completed our shining, glassy other world. Horse and rider could observe the image of perfection they relentlessly strove after.

In the morning I decided to take out a ride of remounts and really have a look around. As *Leopard* trotted down that avenue, bounded by the chestnuts that had now truly flared into full bloom, it seemed to him that horses and men were marching everywhere. Perhaps it amused his stable companions not to have told him yet that Aldershot was the 'hub' of the British Army. We quietly passed the Willems Barracks which now housed the 7th Hussars. It crossed my mind that with two other Cavalry Regiments and the Horse Artillery as companions our life would be much more competitive. Across the main road was that Garrison Church, scene of so many superb Church Parades. On our right we could see the great statue of the Duke of Wellington: what a vast horse, 22 feet 8 inches around the girth, 26 feet from nose to tail, the whole weighing 40 tons. I murmured down to *Leopard,* 'that's the Duke of Wellington on his charger, *Copenhagen,* a chestnut just like you.' *Leopard* fidgeted his bridle slightly, just a little, not impatiently.

On to the Royal Pavilion, residence of any member of the Royal Family when reviewing the troops. Now we were into the open, Long Bottom stretching away to our left, a beautiful sandy training area with gorse on the upper slopes beginning to show their first yellow blooms. In the centre a valley with dozens of fences and 'dummies' waiting for our swords.

A high promontory, 'Caesar's Camp' overlooked the Long Bottom, for Caesar was the first of several conquerors to pitch his tent there. And so to Tweseldown, the racecourse which naturally intrigued my Leopard — nice sandy going where one day he might be asked to have a go steeplechasing.

We continued in a long half circle until we regained the Long Valley, dusty theatre of many a parade — and in spite of the dust it would be our venue for Regimental and Squadron mounted drills. The Duke of Connaught, around 1880, had wisely ordered small copses of trees to be planted strategically to prevent the sand being blown away and disrupting the entire countryside.

Of course, as I've already indicated, *Leopard* soon learned that life in a Cavalry Brigade was highly, indeed fiercely competitive. Apart from steeplechasing and polo there were the important contests in which a soldier could prove his skill in the use of arms: sword, lance, revolver, or, if dismounted, bayonet.

In the Cavalry we had two major opportunities to demonstrate our ability with the first three. First Dummy Thrusting, against just those dummies which so intrigued *Leopard*. This game might seem a little out of date but it would play a big part in *Leopard's* future. The object was to test a competitor simultaneously as horseman and swordsman, and, further, to assess the harmony of horse and rider working as a combined weapon.

Leopard became fascinated by all the practise required to skewer a sack supposed to represent a man. Imagine a small arena of six fences: over the first we make straight for a cavalryman represented by a sack on a long pole, a five inch disc is his lower throat. About sixteen feet short of this dummy *Leopard*, (he quickly learned) must increase speed that I might readily attack and drive the sword well through my opponent. I bring my sword to the engage and as *Leopard* puts on his spurt, turn the blade upwards to facilitate withdrawal — in — out — and almost immediately another opponent on my left. Thank goodness they were only dummies! Over the second brush fence to find an infantryman prone on the ground, a lunge at him and then swing over the next fence (sandbags this time), to attack first an infantryman standing to our right, another kneeling, this latter supported by a cavalryman. Barely time to disengage from the kneeling man, so all I can do is punch

9. ". . . *harmony of horse and rider, working as a combined weapon.*"

10. "*Leopard enjoyed this life. It had many lighter moments.*"

my annoying opposite number with the hilt of the sword.

So it continued until *Leopard* and I had attacked and, hopefully, overcome nine opponents dressed in sackcloth — and mine were the ashes if I hadn't picked up enough marks for our style in the attack.

The other contest involved sword, revolver and lance. Here the cavalryman would ride over a couple of fences successively attacking two dummies with his sword, leaving it in the second of them, draw his revolver and while galloping over a further two fences, burst three balloons (each, of course, representing an enemy), slap the revolver back into the holster and, turning about at the gallop, grasp a lance stuck in the ground to take two rings of no more than 3 inches in diameter followed by a peg. Rings were cavalry opponents, the peg an unfortunate prostrate infantryman.

Many a day did *Leopard* and I practise but, alas and alack and rather to my chagrin, at the Command Championship we were second in each competition to the same officer of the 7th Hussars. My luck was short that year: in practise, punching the cavalryman was my undoing, I bashed him on the iron frame and broke a bone in my hand.

Leopard and I returned to Warburg Barracks a little disappointed. Worse, the idiotic injury meant I couldn't play polo. So the ponies were either lent out or sold. I settled down with renewed determination to the training of *Leopard* and of the Trick Ride.

May Day came and the scene had changed rather dramatically for me thanks to the broken hand. The Trick Ride would now have to be the best thing ever. *Leopard* sensed this, and also that he might have to start show jumping to replace my polo.

Two newcomers had arrived in our stable. *Cully Naxter,* a large dark bay, and a lighter bay called *Mousie.* The first was young and felt some affinity with *Leopard* for he had much to learn, but *Mousie* wasn't slow to tell the others that although only a troop horse he'd won more than once in the show jumping arena.

The Trick Ride gained in professionalism and gradually assumed the pattern which was to become definitive in the next three years. Tent pegging of all kinds dominated the first part, with Sergeant Major Gough, Sergeants Hodgson and Lee and myself as the mainstays of the ride. Apart from pegs we had to pick up handkerchiefs and the like from the ground. The left stirrup strapped to the string girth, the rider would bring his right leg over the horse's head, hook it into the strap which held the left stirrup and, leaning over backwards on the right side, hang down until he could touch the ground — all this at a full gallop. Easy, you might say, but the straps did break and a crash helmet would have come in handy, as I learned myself on one or two occasions.

Leopard enjoyed this life. It had many lighter moments. The sight of my old two-seater Sunbeam coupé, for example, which had to be given a push to start by the dismounted instructors, resplendent in their black jackboots. One afternoon he simply didn't believe his eyes when the Sunbeam drew up before the stables: seated in the back was a horse! But what sort of midget could be sharing the dickie with Rushton? Peat helped him to lift the toy horse out of the Sunbeam. He stood thirty-two inches high. I didn't feel in the least apologetic and explained to Peat that I'd bought this Shetland pony, to be called *Donald*, for only £2.

Leopard had a good look as he was led into the stable, but little guessed what a friendship would be forged.

May and the first half of June were busy for all of us. *Leopard* got to know the entire training area and particularly took to a splendid site of about ten acres furnished with every conceivable obstacle: ditches, water jumps, cut and laid fences, post and rails of every size, even

11. ". . . and now for Show Jumping."

60

a railway with the signal wires that *Leopard* remembered well from his first hunt with the York and Ainsty. A heavenly haven for horses and horsemen, as W. S. Gilbert might have written. In the Riding School he learned the precise detail of his turn in the Trick Ride, together with *Gertie, Greasy* and *Red Lady*, soon to be joined by the diminutive *Donald*, newly clipped out and looking like a little racehorse.

Until the day in mid-June when the evening session came to a sudden end. The Aldershot Tattoo was about to open, which meant that every Officer and Trooper had to be on duty. Even Corporal Samuels, our wonderful bald-headed clown, had to exchange the motley for his smart green livery and silver buttons and attend to his Officers' Mess duties.

From the door of his stable *Leopard* gazed unbelievingly. That square, sacred to the horse and marching men, had become a car park. Unbelievable too, the litter left by the occupants of those cars. It lay there until the familiar call for Fatigues rang out the next morning:

'Come! Now get out — You needn't mind your rig:
This means broom and brushes, don't try and rush it,
Work when on Fatigue!'

Soon we were past the longest day — and suddenly *Leopard* noticed that *Mousie's* and *Sunbeam's* loose boxes were empty. A week later Peat returned with them from Olympia where they'd been competing at the International Horse Show and after their feed Peat opened the glass cases and tacked up a blue rosette in *Mousie's* — our first success at Olympia. *Leopard* looked on enviously. How proud *Mousie* seemed, for although we'd won other rosettes, his was the only blue.

Now training could start up again. Most evenings at about six o'clock Peat went to the School with *Leopard* and *Donald* and I came along accompanied by a beautiful pale whippet named *Jess,* who'd been given to me after winning at Olympia with *Mousie.* Descending in size like the three bears, this trio, *Leopard, Donald* and *Jess,* became the most devoted friends. In the School I would always find Gough, Hodgson and Lee, all working absorbedly. In one corner

61

Rushton concentrated on *Donald* — but they didn't take up much room! Our work was very informal here and that was how new ideas were formed and set in motion.

Like the others, I worked *Leopard* at all paces, building up his trust, certain that so long as he understood what was wanted he would never let me down. We had a number of assorted fences, about three feet six inches and never wider than three feet, always without guiding wings, for our four horses had to become ultra obedient. To begin with, when necessary a couple of the arena party would stand on each side of the fence.

These horses were ridden in plain saddles, double bridles, without martingales but with breast plates we could grab if we had to, so avoiding interference with the horses' mouths. It would have been shameful to retain my balance by giving *Leopard* a jab in the mouth. These evening sessions were fun, sometimes lasting until nine o'clock. Nobody minded missing the evening meal, easy to put that right later with sandwiches and a bottle of beer.

Our ideas multiplied. *Leopard* trusted me so why not try jumping moving fences? A couple of the arena party picked up a short length of rope and walked towards us.

12. ". . . so why not real skipping."

That was too easy — in no time at all *Leopard* realised he would have to take off earlier to be right for the advancing rope, so why not real skipping?

I taught him when to, and when not to jump a spray of water like this: a remount rider would hold his hose about three feet from the ground; as we approached I pushed him on with my legs and he would jump it. Then I turned about and walked or jogged towards the spray, talking to him all the time, keeping my hands pressed down on his withers, not pushing with my legs while checking him from increasing his pace. Like that he remained calm and walked through the water.

Someone thought, why not play "Nuts in May"? So *Leopard, Gertie, Greasy* and *Red Lady* made up one team while five of the arena party came towards us, holding handkerchiefs and singing 'Here we come gathering Nuts In May'. No problems, all four horses took off well away from our youngsters and we jumped between them as they sang. While it went on *Donald* and Rushton and even *Jess* were learning to jump these weird fences too.

Each and every day we became more ambitious. Why not one platform, but that would be too easy, why not one that was on the move? The answer was a strong brewer's dray, covered with matting so that our horses couldn't slip. Who would pull it? *Jerry* of course, our magnificent piebald Drum Horse. But who should drive him, for *Jerry* would undoubtedly consider this job rather beneath his dignity? We solved the problem by asking Trooper Knott, the Forage Orderly, to take him on. *Jerry* now felt pretty sure he would get a bit of extra feed.

When that dray was driven into the School, *Leopard* and his pals seemed a little amazed. What had come over the highly respected Drum Horse, here stripped of his silver drums and embroidered banners? The horses had somehow to be convinced that the dray wouldn't collapse when thirteen or so hundredweight landed on top: it was soon done, they were all confident. We treated the dray as a bus, and though sometimes you might cadge a lift, Daly the clown was usually only too quick to join Trooper Knott and

"*We treated the dray as a bus.*"

13.

collect our fares for him while *Jerry* chugged stolidly on!

Didn't *Leopard* get tired doing all this? Perhaps I could teach him to lie down and take a peaceful nap. After all Army horses had been taught in the Boer war how to lie flat so as to conceal themselves — surely *Leopard* could learn?

First I dismounted, and his near foreleg was strapped up at the knee and a second strap was placed around his off foreleg just below the fetlock joint. I then stood on his left side, gently pulling his head to the right while also pulling on the long strap attached to the off fore fetlock. Peat would now push him on to his left side towards me. I immediately sat on his shoulder and gave him a good pat and some sugar. *Leopard* naturally thought this was not only very easy but a good way to get a rest. Not to be outdone *Donald* rapidly learned to lie down between *Leopard's* legs and snuggle up to him. *Jess* couldn't bear to be left out either and she lay on top of one or the other. In the years to come a quick rest could be of untold value, but there were occasions when they went into this routine unasked — and that could be quite embarrassing!

Evening followed evening, our training flourished and the Officers' Trumpet Call to Dinner as often as not went unheeded:

   'Oh! what a time those Officers have—
   I'd like to have their dinner!
   Just give me theirs and let them have mine
   I'll bet they'll get much thinner!
   They know it, you bet! And don't you forget
   That wine and music's fine to digest,
   And help to season dinner . . .'

Leopard and I were much happier in the school with the others. That August we were engaged to go out on tour. Already we felt akin to those great circuses of the open road, and indeed Bernard Mills had more than kindly allowed Samuels and Daly to stay with him and learn something of the clown's art. For professionalism was our burning ambition. Amateurism already far behind.

CHAPTER 9
On Tour

The canvas battlements, the broken shields, the inadequate armour and blunted swords were all packed away. Our Tattoo over, we must buckle down to serious Military Training. Yet those pageants taught us much. I could never have guessed then the importance of that experience for my future: the tuning of an organisation to such a pitch that it becomes a thing of beauty, the delights of discipline when directed to a productive end.

From early morning till after dusk I rode my four principal horses, *Flying Fish, Cully Naxter, Mousie* and *Leopard*. When instructing, my horses were learning too. While the recruits had a breather and Sergeant Lee talked to them about the care of their charges I sometimes had a fence or two raised and practised around the Mounted Sports ground.

If I were astride *Leopard* I would regularly remind him of his new trick: 'Why not have a rest, lie down?' At first, doubtful that he'd heard right, he would be reluctant until I'd eased his head round to the right by pulling his ear or tapping him gently with my whip on the left cheek — then a little reminder from my foot under his left elbow and down he would go. *Leopard* enjoyed lying on that soft, sandy soil.

The August Bank Holiday loomed nearer and both the Musical and the Trick Rides were going on tour. The former was, of course, established, but it rehearsed two or three evenings a week, while the Trick Ride was still taking shape. After evening stables Maddocks and Almond slipped away down the Wellington Avenue, out into the Long Valley where they straddled their pairs of horses, Cossack fashion, to gallop towards the setting sun. It could have been a film sequence, and quite good enough for one too, but although they enjoyed every minute there were no pennies from heaven for them of course.

"Maddocks slipped away . . . to gallop towards the setting sun."

14.

Later, on the Sports Ground, while the tent pegging and vaulting proceeded, *Leopard* watched on the side lines, attended by *Donald* and, of course, *Jess* the whippet. He'd begun to feel very much the star and as the sun began to spread behind the trees of that superb oasis, his ears pricked a little impatiently, waiting for his cue to enter. Peat would at last take the horse I'd been using for pegging and I mounted *Leopard*. In we went, followed by Rushton 'packing' the diminutive *Donald* into a railway trunk, which in turn was lifted on the dray to be pulled by the noble *Jerry*.

By now *Leopard* was only too happy to lie down at any time — that sweet order meant a rest plus sugar or a carrot — but he felt a trifle ruffled when a new prop, a double bed, appeared one day in the Riding School. Surely he wouldn't be obliged to get into that? His dignity didn't quite fancy the prospect. Great relief then, when he saw the

68

15. *"Why not have a rest, lie down?"*

16. *". . . and both the Musical and Trick Rides were going on tour."*

clowns climb into it and suddenly the order, 'Come on boy,' and away he headed, straight for them. Gosh, he hoped the bed was safe — yes it was — on to the bed and off over the headboard, the two clowns untouched, unmoved, sound asleep having said their prayers!

The day of departure arrived. A special train and what a train! Ten horse boxes (and in his own first class one for six, *Leopard* was amused to find *Mousie* and *Cully Naxter* accompanying them, to compete and earn a few bob in the Show Jumping events) and a minimum of 100 men including the Band. The special, indeed specialised, train drew out of Aldershot to return a week later.

Our first stop, Brewood in Staffordshire. That Thursday evening we detrained in a siding. They'd erected special stabling for us nearby. The train to remain there until we set off again on Sunday morning. Friday, the day of rehearsals, seemed a kaleidoscope and a whirl to *Leopard*. Never had so many lovely young women surrounded him or found so many ways of saying, 'Oh, how beautiful you are, what a nice horse!' And nice things for a nice horse — an ice-cream, a bun, a lump of sugar. There were striking costumes and caps he hadn't seen before, competitors from all the surrounding villages arrived for a gala band contest.

Leopard could hardly be blamed for the 'spoiling' and the 'petting' — and that's what he principally remembered afterwards about Brewood — or for being a little comfort loving (he worked quite hard for his living). So when he arrived at their next stop, Bakewell, he wasn't too pleased to find himself tied in a line with his friends, there being no stables (shades of Catterick). This was barely a one-night stand! They returned to the railway sleeper that night and were off again on the move early next morning.

To Lutterworth: in the heart of the Atherstone hunting country. A small show but memorable for one thing: *Leopard* wasn't sure he'd heard correctly when Peat muttered in his ear, 'Come on my lad, you're going to show jump like *Mousie* and *Cully Naxter* — but you'll be a novice not competing against them two.' Despite his misgivings *Leopard* found the fences easy and finished second, winning

70

17. "You're going to Show Jump."

thirty bob.

Their ultimate destination turned out to be Tring, possibly the greatest of the one-day shows in that era. As a setting, no one could dispute that Tring Park was beautiful and the opportunities to compete were very varied — sheep dog trials, gun dog trials, hunter trials and all the show horse trials in addition to show jumping. And did *Leopard* enjoy the superb stables! He ate his breakfast in peace, gazing at the gently rolling Park spread out before him, savouring in anticipation a long leisurely forenoon peopled with nice, kind folk who gave him oranges, sugar, and even bananas when, down to earth with a jolt! Peat loomed before him with his saddle and bridle.

'Come on lad, good thing I've groomed and smarted you up, the boss has entered you for the Hunter Trials.'

The course proved easy though, along one side of a valley and back the other, fences either simple brush hurdles or post and rails. 'What in the world's the point of this?' thought *Leopard* grumpily to himself. He felt himself even more amazed and astonished when he formed up on the

71

right of the line in the main ring and was presented with a blue rosette.

Hardly had the applause subsided when *Leopard* saw some hounds coming into the arena. What now? He loved hounds and the Huntsman was blowing his horn. Would he be expected to go hunting? Merely part of the show, of course, but it left *Leopard* a bit disappointed. He galloped out, to be met by Peat with 'Well done lad, quick now, we must get you ready for the Trick Ride.' I cannot swear that *Leopard* did think, 'Who says only a woman's work is never done' but a slightly suppressed snort seemed to convey that!

Early next day our private train (for that's what it amounted to) puffed into Aldershot station, *Leopard* glad he'd soon be back with his friends and recounting his adventures to *Flying Fish*. Best of all though, Peat turned to me that evening and said, 'Now we'll have to get him a case for his rosettes!'

'Go ahead, knowing my *Leopard* there'll be many.'

Leopard felt pretty sure he'd earned a short rest after touring around England like a film star. What next — racing perhaps? He rested briefly, while *Fish, John* and one or two others did the recruit and remount rides, but at the end of August the Trick Ride travelled to Manchester to perform in a Tattoo at the giant floodlit Belle Vue stadium.

Little rehearsing to be done this time for the entourage was by now well-knit and fortunately we had our own Inniskilling Band to play the appropriate tunes — *"Thanks for the Buggy Ride"*, as *Leopard* and *Gertie* leapt up on the wagon — *"There' no more money in the Bank"*, *"Let's put out the lights and go to bed"*, when Corporals Samuels and Daly, duly blowing out a large candle, crept into the reinforced double bed on which and over which the equine stars performed.

Autumn drew on. The entire team had retired into well deserved Winter Quarters at Aldershot. Evening sessions in the Riding School faded out, except for little *Donald* and another Shetland pony, *Charlie,* a new recruit generously given to the Ride by the widow of an old clown who had performed at the Belle Vue circus right up to his death.

72

But there was one unexpected stir. *Leopard* listened and watched intently while Peat packed up everything to do with *Mousie* and *Cully Naxter*. He learned that these two were going to jump for their country, for Great Britain, and they were travelling a very long way to somewhere called America and Canada. Major show jumping competitions it seemed, and they were rather puffed out with pride. *Leopard* couldn't decide whether he felt envious or not.

Luxford now took good care of my chosen horse who'd packed a great deal into the past ten months — the hunt of his life with the Middleton, numerous Trick Ride performances, a start at show jumping and hunter trials, and that strangely fated dummy thrusting incident. But for this last *Leopard* might have never blossomed as he did — polo would undoubtedly have taken precedence.

The year ended as Peat returned with *Cully Naxter* and *Mousie* — and a box full of rosettes to join those in the glass cases. I found a host of engagements for the Trick Ride for the coming year, 1932, waiting for me.

CHAPTER 10
Now Racing

January, dark mornings, but the firm of Peat, Turnbull and Luxford were always open in time to feed their horses — so what did *Leopard* care about dark mornings provided he had something to eat?

Reveille sounded at half past five and by seven I'd be down at the indoor school to take the first recruit ride. When I returned to breakfast one morning at about nine I found a message from my commanding officer, Lt. Colonel Roger Evans, asking me to go and see him. The substance of the interview was this: 'Mike, the Regiment has been invited to put on a riding display at the International Horse Show. There have been a few objections, or might I say problems, for the Royal Military Tournament believe they have first call on any military display.' He added, 'What would you like to do?' and without hesitation I said, 'Please may we go to the International Horse Show?'

The answer might have been terse — but a Cavalry Regiment had never been invited before. Hearing of our difficulty, the Earl of Lonsdale apparently went straight to H.M. King George V who immediately gave his consent to our missing the Royal Tournament.

Naturally, the eagerness of my reply showed I was far from disinterested. For various reasons I couldn't afford to start playing polo again and try to regain my position in that world. Being ambitious and determined I'd switched all my spare energies to the Trick Ride and Show Jumping. Now I had my own problem, for I simply had to compete in the Dummy Thrusting and All Arms, which would take place only ten days before the International Horse Show. Further, I knew how *Leopard* was bred and despite all he'd done it felt essential to start him steeplechasing and point-to-pointing. At least Peat had no reservations. When I mulled the matter over with him he came out with a forthright: 'Our *Leopard* can do the "lot".'

'The lot' it was to be. It meant *Leopard* would be running his first race at Tweseldown at the end of March, the Dummy Thrusting at Olympia and returning there almost immediately for the International Horse Show. As we made our plans in the stable, *Leopard* listened with interest.

Evening after evening throughout January and February, *Leopard, Donald* and *Charlie* were in the school, lights ablaze and a gramophone with a large horn blaring out tunes which *Leopard* and I so enjoyed such as, "Daisy, Daisy, give me your answer do". My happy quartet of *Gertie, Red Lady, Greasy* and *Leopard* certainly did give the answer with a vengeance. In one corner, the Shetlands would be flying through hoops, playing leapfrog and learning to lie down as instantaneously as *Leopard*.

We pooled our ideas, consciously 'raised our game' as gamblers say, with the difference that we could not and would not leave anything to chance. Our horses and ponies would be supreme, every one of us silently swore that. Fences became narrower and narrower until we used chairs without arms, jumping without reins. It would all be virtually impossible now. No one has the time or resources.

Our four splendid stars could jump anything. An evening came when one of us looked at the arena party, innocently standing by, and thought, why shouldn't they be sandwich men? Why not indeed? But these boards would advertise nothing, other than silver spurs, crossed swords and a burnished cuirasse — emblems of our cavalry which soon, we knew, but hid from ourselves, must pass into history.

The boards were simply three-ply wood and the gallant

party strode down the arena, lined up in single file, seventeen feet apart, squatted down on their haunches, sank their heads between the board and, I believe prayed to heaven as *Leopard* led the others down the line and over the sandwich boards. In later years the arena party weren't so keen on this act and decided they'd like to form a union. Eventually, but reluctantly, we decided three-ply wood was insufficient armour and the warlike emblems a slightly unkind joke on their bearers so we cut it out. Pity though!

Leopard felt particularly special and sophisticated returning to the stables after these evenings. He would wake up *Fish, Cully Naxter* and his other pals, tell them anything odd that had happened and remind them that, he'd be delighted to breakfast only with his friends, as stars performed late in the evening he must be allowed to rest during the day!

One crisp March morning I took a very smart person around my stables, accompanied by his own grown up son. Almost identical they were, tall and with small black moustaches. The father showed great interest in *Leopard,* asking that he might be led out and his rug removed. Almost immediately he said, 'Why not give him a race?' *Leopard* understood this and thought 'Hell, what next?' I was only too glad to agree, for this smart person was none other than Tom Walls, who was possibly the greatest comedian of those times. He appeared regularly with Robertson Hare, Ralph Lynn, Mary Brough and the attractive Winifred Shotter. Night after night and for some years they filled the Aldwych with laughter. Apart from this fame on the stage he bought and trained horses and achieved renown, being the only owner and trainer to win the Derby at his first attempt. His son had joined the Inniskillings some months earlier and had told his Dad all about *Leopard.*

More than kind, Tom Walls insisted that he really would like to have *Leopard* in training at his home near Epsom for the rest of the month that he might race at Tweseldown.

Peat and I were already prepared for such a problem. *Leopard* would have to be at his best for Dummy Thrusting and All Arms and the International Horse Show — both in

77

June — quite a plateful, but he couldn't possibly miss the oppportunity to be trained by Tom Walls, so I thanked the delightful actor very much.

Peat was delighted. He and *Leopard* would enjoy the change, and surely it was time the son of *Maître Corbeau* did something other than hunt, trick ride, dummy thrust, compete in hunter trials and show jump!

The morning of their departure, after he'd cleaned *Leopard's* saddlery to perfection, Peat approached his favourite, saying: 'Now then, lad, there's a box outside and we're off to make you into a racehorse.'

Destination Racing Stables: When he got there *Leopard* would have liked to have told Peat that he'd never seen anything so splendid. Such lovely loose boxes, painted black with white doors, roofs of red slate. A superb indoor school, and within easy reach there was a short gallop and, of all joy, a sand bath. This last meant that having learned to lie down he could roll about in the sand and revel in the sun — very different from the Aldershot Riding School where the tan always tended to be damp!

Next door to his new home stood a horse called *April the Fifth,* nice looking but quite young, his named painted clearly on the dark woodwork. On his other side the name was *Crafty Alice.* Mm! He brooded a little and secretly began to hope that his name might also be put up — after all he was *Leopard.*

Here the morning routine was more rigorous than in the barracks. An earlier reveille, a feed and then out with eight or nine others, quietly walking to some glorious downs and a canter of about two miles. Perfect, a real holiday this part. Peat enjoyed it too. Then home to a good breakfast followed by the sort of grooming called strapping — really a massage.

Mid-morning that smart gentleman would arrive. Smart, perhaps, but he was no gentleman of leisure and he knew everything. He strolled around, meticulously appraising each horse, and finally came to *Leopard.*

'Well, dear lad, d'you know who is standing next to you? This is my *April the Fifth* and if you had any money I'd tell you to back him for the Derby.'

That puzzled *Leopard,* what did he know about the Derby? And Mr. Walls continued in the same amused, bantering tone, '*Crafty Alice* there, on your other side, she can jump and I want my son to win the Grand Military Gold Cup on her.

Leopard felt rather shy, he didn't understand all this. But he understood all right when a little later Peat brought him out and they were led to a lane of fences. *Leopard* knew all about this particular sort — a loose lane leading, with luck, to a good handful of oats. His luck was in, oats were plentiful.

Day followed day in this pattern until *Leopard* felt almost drugged by the perfection of his life. But a couple of times a week Peat stirred him up with 'The boss is coming to gallop you today — soon we must get busy with Dummy Thrusting and the Trick Ride.'

Sure enough, at the end of three weeks *Leopard* heard that he must return to Military Duties. He bade farewell to *April the Fifth* (who did in fact win the Derby that year) and assured *Crafty Alice* that he would certainly see her again as her boss was also in the Inniskillings. That came true too. But, it was truly farewell to those lovely red roofs, the carefully raked gravel, the sparkling sand, the early morning gallops over Epsom Downs.

Leopard had felt so confused, so upset without quite knowing why, that he'd hardly been conscious of Peat leading him into the motor horsebox. He didn't look back, he made little of the shapes out of focus as they passed on the road until — but surely that looked like Aldershot? And to his astonishment, they shot by the Warburg Barracks, straight past *Copenhagen* and the Duke of Wellington. Well, the driver must be lost, he didn't know the way. On down the road they went, leaving the dummies on the left, climbed past the Mounted Sports Ground till they were up on the Tweseldown racecourse.

When *Leopard* was led over to some rather crude stalls and caught sight of me he felt reassured: but a shade of puzzlement passed through him again seeing me hand a very light saddle to Peat, with a cloth holding some lead. Quickly saddled up, Peat threw a lightweight rug over him — welcome on that bleak hill in March. Then, straight into the enclosure to be led round with eleven other horses. A bell rang, and I came over to my protégé who was amazed to see me for the first time in a blue jersey with orange sleeves and cap. Peat gave me a leg up while *Leopard* wondered why the riders wore such a variety of colours. A troop horse race this, but my *Leopard* was no ordinary troop horse.

Out of the paddock with a 'good luck' pat from Trooper Peat, a rapid order to line up from a man on the rostrum, down went his flag and away we went, fast for the first fence. Easy, *Leopard* well up with the first five. On at a steady gallop, turn right over the road, well covered with earth, then a large open ditch. Two more fences down the hill and *Leopard* felt himself being pushed along in the lead. Another right turn at the bottom and then back up the hill through a cutting. Now to get a breather, no hurry here, going up hill, no place to make up ground, let the others try. A right hander on good flat going and once again down that hill. Now I was really pushing my *Leopard,* well placed, one other horse with us, but I knew he had plenty in hand. Round the top right bend again and only one more fence before the run in. *Leopard* just walked away from his fellow troop horses, winning his first ever race with ease.

We pulled up quietly. 'Well done, old boy!'

Back in the enclosure, *Leopard* took little notice of the crowd of friends and admirers until he suddenly came on Peat — and that dour Yorkshireman certainly looked well pleased.

So, a first race won and in fine style. But no smart horsebox now for our rising star. Peat just got up and rode him

". . . winning his first race ever with ease."

18.

back to barracks, neither of them sure which was the prouder.

When I returned in my old Sunbeam, *Jess* sitting up beside me, her courser lines stretched and taut as though she'd won a race and was prepared to run another for as long as anyone liked — I went immediately to the stable. Peat, Turnbull and Luxford were supposed to be cleaning saddlery, but it was hard to keep at that with a victor there waiting for tokens of their admiration. I joined them and tried to tell *Leopard* how big was my 'thank you'.

Lights were soon out. No practise for the Trick Ride tonight! I went up the steep stone stairs to my quarters, turned on the gas fire, had a hot bath and then went to the Mess for a celebration. I felt, in that absurd way one does sometimes, that the whole world should celebrate with me.

CHAPTER 11
The Royal Military Tournament

In bed that night one thought circled in my head and would not leave: I must get my priorities right. Like successive shooting stars the projects flared down — Dummy Thrusting and All Arms, Royal Military Tournament, International Horse Show. The second star could only follow the first and though *Leopard* and I simply had to win with the sword we would simultaneously be rehearsing, relentlessly, for the Horse Show.

Naturally, I also had Regimental duties, which meant a deal of dovetailing to make the most of every hour. I would ride *Leopard* while giving morning instruction to the recruits and remounts so that during their 'easy' I could go and practise Dummy Thrusting under the scrutiny of Sergeant Major Gough. And that reminds me of a curious detail — a year later when I became Adjutant I remember being intrigued to find a paragraph in the secret Mobilisation Orders saying that, in the event, all swords would immediately be returned to the armourer for sharpening! Mine would hardly have needed that as the Armourer had sharpened it like a razor for the Dummy Thrusting. *Leopard* and I practised every morning with that weapon and although I'm only too thankful never to have gone to war with a horse, this sword drill imbued us all, Troopers and Officers alike, with the necessary offensive, aggressive spirit: engage, attack, withdraw.

Day after day we would practise around that delightful green oasis of trees and grass with the sandy area stretching away lit by clumps of bright gorse. Ample space for Trick Ride rehearsals, Dummy Thrusting and for *Cully Naxter* to train for Show Jumping.

My ambition was planning, in order that thereby the Inniskillings would leap into the same class as the famed Cadre Noir of Saumur and the Spanish Riding School from Vienna. That was something and I swear that *Leopard,* as he nearly always did, knew what we were striving for. The two parts of the Ride had become well set — first the tent pegging, vaulting, the Cossack riding and the tumbling clowns, then after the interval we put on what was beginning to be a surprising display of dazzling jumping. Each evening our four stars, *Gertie, Leopard, Red Lady* and *Greasy,* assembled in the indoor school. The Bandmaster with his gramophone would never miss an evening, the Regimental Tailor, and, of course, the Master Saddler appeared frequently to fit on the costumes, their new saddles and try out new ideas. Enthusiasm was so high that we never had to ask for volunteers to join the arena party — every man in the Regiment wanted to be part of the Show.

Every time *Leopard* approached that well lit Riding School he wondered what else he could possibly be asked to learn. He had his moments of being, not blasé exactly, it was just that he'd begun to feel so very much a professional. 'Those little brick walls, three feet six inches high by twelve inches wide, 16 in a straight line, placed at a distance, allowing for no stride in between, Lor' bless you, I could sail over those in the dark.' Perhaps he could.

'Pairs of those tiddlers eighteen feet apart? — just you watch *Gertie* and me! *Red Lady* and *Greasy* follow and if you think they look quite as good as us, well they still have to follow us don't they? And when they stick 'em in line, 16 only nine feet apart, no room for a stride between, yes I do feel like missing out a few now and then but, oh well, I suppose it's my training and I don't want to let the old man down, so I don't. Anyway, I like to make it look easy, we've

84

all got our pride haven't we?'

What next now? The arena party and our clowns have all worked hard so I suppose they expect a meal? Right, a meal of sorts it shall be. So we'd bring on a few tables especially made which were pretty strong — they had to be, for although *Leopard* would clear them in one leap and *Gertie* or *Red Lady* jump on and straight off, *Greasy* had a way of lingering among the crockery. This last was fortunately fairly cheap in those days for we knew what would happen once everyone had sat down to table, each laid with a beautiful white cloth, laden with succulent delicacies, untouched till the clowns discovered they were made of papier maché, then there was an explosion. *Gertie* and *Red Lady* might break a plate or two but *Greasy* was always determined to appear Bolshie or as we now say, militant; he'd leap on to each table in turn smashing every single piece that remained intact until a volley of smacks from the dinner guests forced him to go on his way.

The ideas came but the trouble with having ideas is that you constantly feel you've got to have a new one. What to do with *Leopard* next? He could jump anything with or without reins so why bother to put on a bridle? Logical, but I felt we'd better still have some control, at least to start with.

These four horses were always ridden with double bridles and breast plates but no martingales. I soon found that if I tied a silk handkerchief or a piece of soft hide over his tongue and around his bottom jaw, with a length of string attached, you could dispense with bridle and bit.

We tried it. *Leopard's* silk handkerchief proved very inexpensive for he never tore it and we painted the bit of string to match his chestnut colouring — so nobody in the audience could imagine it was there. When we four horsemen cantered into the arena with all the panache we could muster and had circled a few times before undoing the throat lashes and slinging our bridles over to the arena party, spectators were electrified. No one spotted the strings, but I confess I didn't then realise that in twelve months' time we wouldn't bother with strings or handkerchiefs.

Our four stars now shone brightly. Our sole concern now was to provide a production that would ensure their being recognised as the four great experts they were.

April ended, and so little time to June when Olympia would be the stage for our two great trials.

In those days every Regiment was still self-contained in a way that might be considered feudal, I suppose, by some people now. That is to say we had our own experts in every craft and trade; all were kept busy and they certainly had to use their own imagination. Our enthusiastic Lt. Colonel Roger Evans and his wife Eileen would arrange Sunday luncheon parties for talented guests who might afterwards be expected to lend a hand painting the many and varied props. Sandwich boards emblazoned with their crests and emblems, brick walls that looked convincing with moss or even aubretia growing in the cracks.

Another idea was when we all wore scarlet tights, green cloaks lined with yellow (the regimental colours) and dashing Robin Hood headgear bedecked with feathers. The Robin Hood Ride! And the name stuck.

Night after night we practised, narrower and narrower the jumps. Because of the effort and stress *Leopard* and I now understood each other more than ever. With only a thread and a silk handkerchief between us I soon learnt that by using the breastplate and pressing on his withers just in front of the saddle, I could, if I used my legs correctly, signal exactly what I wanted of him.

Soon after May Day *Leopard* found himself close to that crucial challenge which, if we won, would take him to the Royal Military Tournament. *Cully Naxter* came too and approaching the now familiar Mounted Sports Ground they nodded to each other sagely: all these motor cars honking and horses milling around — something was definitely on!

'A race, could it be?' wondered *Leopard,* 'but if so why's this blooming sword flapping against my left flank?' They turned off through the gate and *Leopard* blinked a little more rapidly as he saw the crowd and heard the rise and fall of the buzzing voices. But soon he calmed down when he realised that the more elderly gentlemen in red hatbands were only Generals, they meant no harm.

When I arrived I found *Leopard* outwardly calm but could sense that he felt this would be one of his days. And truly it was so: when *Leopard* saw a judge on a shooting stick beside each of the dummies he determined that no red disc should go unstuck! I certainly felt the same. We could do no wrong. I felt it the first time round, each disc driven through, out and away. We won that and when we followed with the 'sword, lance and revolver' I felt like a conjuror pulling rabbits out of a hat, it seemed so easy. One doesn't often get such days. The stable was on a winning streak for *Cully Naxter* jumped a clear round and Sergeant Hodgson won both events for Non-Commissioned Officers. Banzai! as the Japanese shout, now for my next two shooting stars!

Back at home *Leopard* got a bit of a shock one day rehearsing for our big show. We'd wondered what to do with our break when the arena party were changing the props for the second part, and suddenly hit on the idea of having a mock fight with swords: Gough riding *Gertie* against me on *Leopard*. Well padded with fencing jackets and head masks we set to with our sabres, *Leopard* circling and manoeuvring, while he wondered at the clash of steel overhead until — could it be? — he above had nudged him in the left elbow, his head was being gently eased to the right. Well, *Leopard* didn't feel at all tired, but down he must go, so down he went. For a few awful moments he believed it must be defeat and not a trick, for I lay as if dead on top of him, Gough and *Gertie* had jumped him and Gough had struck his sabre through my back. This, then, was the end of the world. *Donald,* led by Rushton came in carrying a wreath — at least he might get a consolatory nibble. But just as *Donald* had dropped the lovely flowers on him and lain between his legs — sympathy indeed ! — *Leopard* received a gentle kick and was up, the master on his back. Ah well, thought *Leopard,* even if the joke's on me I shall know next time.

We needed some more short turns and the three Shetland ponies were just the job. *Jerry* came nobly trundling in pulling his brewer's dray, now doing service as a Railway

19. *"Leopard did not feel a bit tired, but down he must go so down he went."*

20. *". . . towing a surfboard with Samuels hanging on spread-eagled. The gramophone blared 'Life on the ocean wave'."*

Delivery cart, bringing three old-fashioned trunks labelled 'To Kensington Station'. The arena party lifted these down and proceeded to unpack ponies. *Leopard* and I enjoyed watching the three little ones jump. *Charlie* was the naughtiest, quite often taking time off to have a quick nip or kick at Rushton — no doubt habits picked up in his act with the Belle Vue Circus.

Ponies were all very fine but *Leopard* couldn't help feeling that it was about time he, *Gertie, Red Lady* and *Greasy* appeared again. The ponies at last were taking their bow, on with the Quartet. But no, in lumbered *Jerry's* understudy once more at a shambling gallop with Daly the clown astride, towing a surfboard with Samuels hanging on spreadeagled. As it swung in and out of the corners, going as fast as they could, the gramophone blaring "Life on the Ocean Wave", Samuels was lucky not to get his chin bashed in and much else besides!

June came at last, if not flaming, quite warm enough and *Leopard* soon found himself in a horsebox again with *Cully Naxter* and after about an hour he heard Peat saying, 'Well my lad, we are now in London.' And soon they turned into a nice green park and then drew up at some barracks. *Leopard* was no longer a new boy, no longer agog at everything he saw but my goodness was this regiment smart. But these trooopers hurrying around wore scarlet tunics and silver helmets like those he'd seen in the Musical Ride but these had gleaming armour on their chests and backs as well! And he gradually realised all the horses were black.

Leopard alternately munched his hay and dozed, he heard the familiar trumpet calls — he knew them all — then 'Lights Out'. He wondered how long he'd be kept from *Fish* and *Gertie* and all his friends, for he really preferred a country life to this. 'Not this place for me', he thought.

A good feed early next morning, Peat always seemed to give him an extra good one the first morning away, *Leopard* noticed — one of the consolations for being pushed about the place. But when let outside and hearing me say to Peat, 'You must be away by ten', *Leopard's* rejoinder, though silent, came, 'Not much time to digest my meal!' However, for the moment *Leopard* and I went out of the main gate, across the road and into the park around which ran a lovely sandy track. *Leopard* and I thought this perfect, trees everywhere, a great variety of horses, a stretch of water with long thin rowing boats, nurses wheeling prams, almost too much to look at, and safe from that noisy smelly traffic.

Back to the stable for a good drink and a small feed: now Peat really got to work, *Leopard* must look his best today. He plainly didn't enjoy his journey to Olympia. A slippery road and taxis and those furious looking buses came unbelievably close. Still, safe with Peat.

Olympia swarmed with soldiers and men in blue. Line upon line of burnished guns and shining motor-cycles. From his corner *Leopard* could see a large indoor riding school with rows and rows of empty seats. He supposed they'd fill up later. In the corridors, many recruiting stands sought to entice the young to join one of the services, Army, Navy and Air Force competing with various promises of an exciting and glamorous future. *Leopard* really didn't think much of this place and was obviously glad to see me arrive.

The ritual of saddling up completed Peat led him over to a small outside ring where I mounted and trotted round. At last my name was called and when Peat with a friendly pat, said 'Go and stick the lot,' *Leopard* had not time to decide whether the 'lot' referred to the judges or the sacks!

No ordinary riding school, he thought, as he entered the ring, the sun shining down through the glass roof. Few spectators but many officials in the arena, judges, men in charge of the jumps, time keepers, and, of course, those foolish men in sacking, waiting to be stuck!

On our way then. Through that Cavalryman, over that jump, down with the infantry man, and just time to punch that cavalryman on my left with my sword hilt. In no time at all it was over, each and every sack-clothed soldier stuck.

We won the bronze medal. Only partially satisfied, for I felt I might have served *Leopard* better, I told Peat the same for tomorrow and he took him back through the traffic to Knightsbridge Barracks.

All Arms using my sword, revolver and lance, on the

following day had an almost identical procedure. Again we won a bronze medal but we were satisfied.

Riding *Cully Naxter* the next two nights in the Show Jumping, I felt a very changed atmosphere and the arena was packed with eager spectators. Military bands marched and played, the Royal Horse Artillery performed their famous Musical Drive, but most exciting to me were the teams from the Royal Navy and the Marines racing with their guns over walls and even a mock river. Never a dull moment and the Tournament was certainly conducted in high military fashion, backcloths depicting fortresses or battlements, military bands thundering non-stop, the Royal Box packed with generals — all helped to intensify the keen competition.

Cully and I competed in the Prince of Wales' Officers' Individual Championship. So near and yet so far — we only finished second. I would love to have heard *Cully* and *Leopard* discussing their silver and bronze medals. Well pleased, we returned to Aldershot.

CHAPTER 12
International Horse Show 1932

As I drove home with *Jess,* naturally I thought of the International Horse Show, which was to be held at the same place within a fortnight. Though surely the setting and atmosphere would be rather more elegant. Time was running out and still much to plan and rehearse. But, *Leopard* and I had had a good reconnoitre. How often had I thought of that old axiom 'time spent on reconnaissance is never wasted?'

London was too hot and noisy but home could offer us little rest or recreation: I knew it, *Leopard* and *Cully* knew it, or at least felt it. Ten tight days stretched before us, we on the Aldershot end of the pulley that would yank us back to Olympia. We had such high hopes for our Robin Hood Ride and knew that our finesse must match the renowned elegance of the International Horse Show.

A bustle of activity in the Regimental Tailor's Shop — he'd been asked to fashion three small dummies, each to be fitted with miniature Robin Hood costumes, and atop the little felt saddles, specially made by the saddler, they would bob along on our ponies, *Donald, Charlie* and *Jeremy.* No stuffed shirts these, their reins of elastic made them almost prance like marionettes to the movement of the ponies.

Early one morning Peat shouted to Turnbull that they must go to the Quarter-Master's store and draw some green trousers and singlets — until that time only Officers and Sergeants had the privilege of wearing green trousers. They found the entire arena party drawing them, and how right that seemed for the Robin Hood myth has the strongest hold on an English imagination: for did he not dress his freemen in Lincoln Green, lost in the paradise of Sherwood Forest?

Leopard was intrigued for each evening session seemed to bring a surprise. New fences — were they fences? Sixteen trim box trees clipped to a point in yellow tubs, side by side, that's fine, looking like a fence, but now they have been moved into one long line, each trim tree to be jumped on its own. Perhaps I'd better go round? Oh well, *Cully* always says 'trust the master' so down the line we go!

The broom handle really flummoxed him for a bit. A long one, six or seven feet, suspended over a fire. Or was it? Fire no longer had terrors for him, even when the daft arena party did spill paraffin all over the grass! Doubts were justified: some joker had painted a box to look like a hearth, while flames of red and orange ribbon shot up, blown by a fan in the infernal regions beneath. Very realistic, too, but why the broom handle? Bemused, *Leopard* watched *Greasy* slowly approach the blaze, Sergeant Lee aboard. He jumped, Lee grabbed the broom to swing up and catapult away while *Greasy* cantered off on his own. All right so far, but I told him to do it faster. He fairly galloped this time, up

— a sharp crack — the handle had snapped and Lee was flat on his back. Luckily unhurt in the soft tan.

I was elated as I knew we'd found a good finale, but decided we'd have no broom sticks for a witches' sabbath, four trapeze bars would hang from the roof instead. Safety Regulations demanded wire, they wouldn't allow rope, and we feared they might force us to use a safety net. Thank goodness we escaped that.

A few days later *Leopard* couldn't make it out. He and the other horses weren't needed any more. His nose twitched over the stable door as he watched the fences being assembled on the square. The arena party laid out props, the Bandmaster took notes, and riders ran through their turns — on flat feet! *Leopard* stamped the floor impatiently, it was so obvious! The riders ran through the sequence of changing the turns. He should be there — Over and over again, but always the riders were on their flat feet? *Leopard* was so put out he went off his food that night, possibly for the first time.

The mystery cleared, *Cully* or one of the others tipped him the wink — they were only rehearsing — and now Peat and Turnbull got busy trimming them all. 'No long hair in our ride'. The ponies too, manes tightly clipped, tails pulled and all reshod. All received a spare set of shoes and so that the riders shouldn't feel out of it, each was presented with another pair of scarlet tights.

June in the thirties seemed invariably glorious. One glowing day the ride formed up ready to entrain at our familiar Aldershot station. That didn't worry *Leopard*, he'd come to expect first class horse travel! In he went, first, followed by *Cully Naxier* and *Mousie*, then *Gertie, Red Lady* and *Greasy* — all stars in his carriage — six and quite enough too in a first class compartment! Quick that journey, *Leopard* thought he recognised Kensington where they halted, this the station for Olympia. Scores of horses would detrain there during the coming week or so, the era of luxurious motor-hauled horse boxes would have to wait awhile yet.

Leopard had a quick sniff around then nuzzled up to

95

Cully, whispering, 'Surely we've been here before?' Oh yes, but then he went in by the back door, now he was led round to the front! And what a change: a long wide corridor, about fifteen loose boxes on either side, green with white doors. His cup of joy filled to overflowing when Peat brought him something to drink: what a bucket! It was wooden, gleaming white inside, green with yellow hoops on the outside. 'That' thought *Leopard,* 'is a vessel fit for the like of me'. Even the feed tins were burnished bright. But although Trooper Knott already moved about mixing the evening feeds *Leopard* thought it odd that the place seemed very empty — just men hurrying by with hammers, brooms, paint pots and brushes. Where were the spectators? Still, jolly comfortable if rather hot.   Peat brushed him over. 'You won't need a rug but we must keep you smart' and he draped our hero in a linen sheet, green with yellow and scarlet edging. 'Ay, and what's more my lad, you like me are provided with two of everything, one to be worn, t'other at the wash!'

So *Leopard* settled for the night in this heaven-sent comfort. Men arranging the shrubs extended his dessert course, with a lump of sugar, cake, sometimes cheese. It didn't matter which, *Leopard* liked the lot!

As always stable guards watched over them and also the saddlery hanging in the saddle rooms. Two of them on duty for a two hour stretch, smarter even than usual in well-pressed green slacks, pale green singlets and, symbol of their authority, white haversacks. Brooms and forks with their scrubbed white handles and shining prongs stood out more prominently, decorating the picture as lights dimmed and night fell on a typical cavalry scene. I loved that scene. All soldiers and officers were proud and fond of their horses.

Next morning *Leopard* found himself in the main street being led, to his surprise, round to the back entrance. He recognised those rather uncomfortable quarters he and *Cully* had used before. Beyond the main doors into the arena he espied men putting up flags, arranging flowers and raking the tan. My goodness, what a difference! A solid bank of blue hydrangeas reared up at the far end, and down the sides men were planting a narrow bed of nemesia and petunias, these in turn being edged with turf. The Royal Horse Artillery would have swung into that a couple of weeks ago, and what indeed would Samuels and Jerry do with their surfboard act? Up to the right floated more flowers surrounding the Royal Box with rows and rows of gold chairs in front. These of course would be for the important visitors, there were no V.I.P.s in them days!

No rehearsal that first morning, but everyone practised and then most of the men disappeared carrying towels, bound for the Hammersmith Swimming Baths. In the evening, after a full rehearsal, *Leopard* eyed Turnbull and his companions as they filed off to enjoy London. Peat had volunteered to stay; he and the guard filled water buckets, gave the horses another small feed, filled their haynets and then went to bed. So comfortable, mused *Leopard,* but getting hotter.

Dress rehearsal passed in something of a haze for *Leopard* but on opening day his impressions cleared. While Peat groomed him to perfection he concentrated on people arriving. Not many that afternoon, but by the evening they crowded through the doors. Some very enthusiastic persons were shouting, 'Programme, Programme, Opening Night Programme,' and their vivid red uniforms always caught his eye as they weaved back and forth. He'd never seen anything like the new arrivals, ladies in wonderfully coloured long dresses accompanied by gentlemen like unimaginably slender penguins with white ties and top hats. They wandered down the avenue of green stables, nodding and laughing, some even offered *Leopard* a lump of sugar but Peat didn't like this and quietly, a little embarrassed, asked them not to. Soon, except for the odd one or two passing by, all was still again. Stillness punctuated by spasmodic clapping in the distance.

The movement was unbroken. A man dressed in white tie and tails, with a megaphone, called the number of the next horse before his predecessor had left the ring and applause died down. Obviously an International Competition, but for Officers only.

Now appeared two flat drays, like that pulled by *Jerry* but in this case drawn by a pair, each with a postillion in yellow,

". . . groomed him to perfection."

21.

for this was the livery of the Earl of Lonsdale, President of the Show. Back they came, laden with fences and the Ring Guard sounded his posthorn. Time for *Leopard* and his friends to walk round to the big collecting ring. Peat led *Leopard* to the end, alongside *Gertie, Red Lady* and *Greasy*. The stars would enter last.

I went over and patted *Leopard* before mounting *Bill*, my tent pegging horse, fitted with a large saddle so that Gough, who pegged equally well with either hand, could sit behind me and then we'd take two pegs at a time, he on the left, I on the right.

Both doors were flung open and we entered to a crash of

music followed by the vaulters and Maddocks with Almond riding Cossack fashion. Through the bright gap *Leopard* could see an arena lit by beautifully draped chandeliers. Each time I came out Turnbull would frantically knock the pegs from my lance — or check my girths, particularly if we were to pick up handkerchiefs or coloured flags from the ground.

In went *Jerry* at a good gallop, ridden by Daly, with his fellow bald-headed clown Samuels clinging to the surfboard for dear life. Would they skid into the flowers? No matter, the floral decorators had to have something to do next morning. Meanwhile Gough and I slipped on our padded jackets and fencing masks and *Leopard* knew his turn had come. *Jerry* thundered back, the great doors closed for a few seconds and then we were on. *Leopard* had just time to see a packed house and the Royal Box ablaze with colour before the clash of steel as sabre met sabre, forward and back and round, until that gentle nudge at his elbow and *Leopard* knew we'd lost. Down we both went, presumed dead, and *Gertie* jumped over us while Gough gave me a final thrust. Perfectly still I whispered to *Leopard* as we listened to the soft sad music, then little Donald came in to lay that very edible wreath. Lights down, *Leopard* rose to his feet and as we left through the one door *Jerry* emerged from the other dragging his scarlet dray, Knott in his dark green livery, to deliver the railway trunks to Rushton and Donald.

"Gertie jumped over us."

22.

Outside *Leopard* was being rubbed down while Gough and I gladly removed the protective clothing in which we'd sweltered.

The doors flew open again and at a call from the post horn the band began to play and we the four stars, *Leopard, Gertie, Red Lady* and *Greasy* cantered round the ring so that *Red Lady* and *Greasy* might become accustomed to those resplendent spectators. Our arena party took a well earned rest, sitting down to their meal — and soon the fun started. Over the tables, on and off the tables, till the last cup and plate were smashed. On came the eight bearing sandwich boards, down they bobbed saying their prayers, and ne'er a mistake as the four of us jumped in Indian file. In came the clowns putting themselves to bed and to sleep as the quartet jumped on and off their bed. The clowns were safe enough under a wooden quilt!

Now for the coup de théâtre: the tempo slowed, I gave a signal and easing into a canter we undid the throat lashes and all four discarded our bridles. No one could see the handkerchiefs and strings as bridleless we leaped down the lines of narrow walls and over the shrubs trimmed to a point — never once did we make an error. Finally the fake fire was brought in, the lights faded again, and when the fans started up spectators were distracted by what appeared to be a roaring furnace — and few noticed the trapeze bars being lowered from above the chandeliers, while we lined up for our finale in that fearsome light. We rode for the blaze, our horses rose, we caught the bars and swung up among the chandeliers, whilst *Leopard* with a squeal and a gentle buck cantered for the exit with his pals. Thunderous applause.

Leopard soon settled to his routine. Morning exercise in the London streets before any motor cars had appeared. Then a peaceful wait, sometimes munching, while the crowds gradually built up through the day.

23. *"We swung up among the chandeliers."*

Our star quartet kept us on our toes and gave us a surprise or two. They knew that once the fire came on they'd soon have a chance to run free. Setting out on their fire ride they felt like racing for it — *Leopard* knew he shouldn't do it really, but *Red Lady* did love it so and Hodgson found he was going so fast he only just managed to grab the bar with one hand, swung out, nearly left his arm behind and came down with a jolt.

Leopard's growing string of admirers came to see him, often more than once, and he wondered how the ladies stayed so cool and lovely while our men were beginning to droop in the mounting heat that summer. He began to feel homesick, this was indeed a long stay. Then one day, late in the week, several of the staff hurried about anxiously giving instructions, the avenue between the green stables was roped off and there the Earl of Lonsdale waited to greet Their Royal Highnesses, The Duke and Duchess of York, accompanied by Princess Elizabeth. I wish *Leopard* could have known that he gazed at a future King of England and two future Queens that day.

When our gay quartet cantered out of the arena on the last day for the last time they were immediately brought back to join the others, much to their surprise. All riders had dismounted and joining hands they ringed the riderless horses. The audience rose, a flourish of trumpets came and, softly at first, eddying out to a tremendous roar, breakers of sound made the chandeliers ring as everyone sang Auld Lang Syne. Then, all at once, the circle broke, the huge doors were flung back to show a line of London Bobbies waiting for them as *Leopard* and his gang, *Jerry* and our trio of ponies, with others following like wild horses on the plain, galloped from the arena, bucking and shrilly neighing their farewell to tumultuous applause.

CHAPTER 13
The Royal Command Performance

Aldershot and military duties may have seemed a trifle tame to *Leopard* after that trip to London, the attention and petting which are the spoils of success. But he liked routine and a rest, and then there was that march to Tidworth.

We set off early one August morning, nearly three hundred mounted men, trekking quite easily through Basingstoke and Andover, down the now chock-a-block petrol trails and motorway. Only fifty years ago. Those unaffected by progress sometimes say complacently that the 19th Century was the era of Railways and Steamships while our 20th Century is the age of Motor Cars and Aeroplanes forgetting perhaps, that for a time Railways cleared many of the roads for walkers and horsemen. In a small country of course that couldn't last. Anyway, *Leopard* enjoyed those marches.

Once on Salisbury Plain the days became very pleasant and interesting for him. The High Command's current obsession was this: war clouds were massing, aeroplanes would emerge from those clouds, all troop movements must be at night. *Leopard* knew little of and cared less for tactics, but he liked the long 'at ease' as the Summer sun slowly lowered when he and *Flying Fish* in the shade of some small copse waited and munched, while Peat and his friends were digging for rabbits. Then dark, and Peat's gruff 'Come on you two, rest in the day, now's your night duty'.

Moving like that for a month or so, all over the Plain. Then the tedious march for home, via Marlborough through Savernake Forest, still during the night. *Leopard* thought it sad, no peering over hedges, but coolness was lovely and, keeping to the lanes and side roads, no glaring headlights. And where were the flies?

The fame of Robin Hood's Ride had travelled far. There were offers from Belfast once more, Jersey and even Brussels. This last because King Albert was Colonel-in-Chief of the Regiment and, indeed, a Belgian has always been so since Princess Charlotte's day.

Now was the time to demonstrate my ultimate 'coup', as we'd envisaged during our training and preparation. Peat didn't question that he should clean and burnish those resplendent double bridles but *Leopard,* though grateful needed no embellishments.

For I'd found that by the mere pressure of my hands on *Leopard's* withers, using my legs, he knew what was wanted and so away with bridles! Lucky bridles went back to the store room but fences began to be more difficult. Fences? One of his Master's swords stuck in the ground, that was three feet nine inches and yet nothing solid to look at, and eight of them in a line. We must do as we're told, thought *Leopard,* or, as they say, asked.

Early in the New Year we'd learned that King George and Queen Mary would be visiting Aldershot in the Spring. His Majesty had especially asked that he might have the opportunity of seeing the four already renowned stars of the Inniskillings. His Majesty had further expressed a wish to see not only the four great luminaries but also those smaller, twinkling stars, *Donald, Jeremy* and *Charlie.*

The Royal Party would view this short display from the balcony in the Regimental Riding School. Very good, no problem that cannot be overcome. Swords would be a little difficult to see so we acquired some tin basins, regimental issue, soldered three feet six inch pipes to them which, when painted white and filled with tow, blazed like candles.

Our miniatures learnt to retrieve like Labradors. First a

bag of sugar on the end of a string was thrown a few yards: *Donald* and *Charlie* liked sugar all right but it always seemed to lead back to their Master, Trooper Rushton. No complaints, even when the sugar was, for some reason, replaced by a stuffed pheasant smothered in treacle!

Jerry the Drum Horse had never failed to be as pleased as punch taking any part. For this Command Performance he had new clothes and elephant's head and trunk, two pairs of elephant trousers and, perched atop, a highly ornate howdah complete with canopy, from which our clowns, Daly and Samuels, loftily looked down on the world, turbanned and blazing with jewels. These Maharajahs flourished their muskets and after two or three loud bangs the pheasant fell to the ground, retrieved by one or both of the ponies — if both a slight tug of war ensued. *Jerry* was a novel kind of King's Jester — we hoped!

As January merged into February *Leopard* began to wonder if the pattern of his life had changed for good. Mornings without a bridle, watching and demonstrating to these young horsemen, evenings taken up with this theatrical stuff — it was all very well, but what about those happy days with *April The Fifth* and *Crafty Alice* in the flower-bedecked stables? Would he never hunt again? Couldn't he race sometimes?

Here we had a problem. He'd been entererd for a race at Hawthorne Hill in April on a Saturday, and the King's visit would be the following Wednesday. Could we risk racing him? I decided to postpone a decision until after a steeplechase at Tweseldown in March. *Leopard,* at any rate, began to feel again that 'God's in his heaven and all's right with the world' for early, three or four mornings a week, Peat would now say to him, 'Come on boy, today you must wear this snaffle bit so you can have a good pull, on your training gallop. You couldn't get that without your bridle, would you? So you can forget about them flaming candles and all that lark until tonight.'

Leopard enjoyed his pull and his gallop, my goodness, didn't he, and went on to win with ease at Tweseldown.

I talked to Peat the evening after that race as we looked

over the old boy — old already in experience, not in age. Could he honestly be expected to compete on that Saturday, four days before playing the lead in the Trick Ride by Royal Command? He had no understudy and so we'd have a double catastrophe if anything terrible happened in the steeplechase. Peat hardly hesitated. Of course *Leopard* could do both — and more.

Tweseldown was always a bit cold and bleak but Hawthorne Hill, an attractive small course, had nice warm stands and good stabling. The Guards Brigade steeplechases were scheduled for this day and spectators vied with each other in smartness. I hoped, no I believed, *Leopard* would win, and what a double success we'd have on Wednesday!

Eleven starters, we were well away. Tucked in behind the first bunch of three I knew *Leopard* was feeling well, a good steady pull on my hands. A quarter of a mile from the finish I pushed him along, we were soon up with the leaders and approaching the last fence I was clearly ahead. I felt I had the race won and then, like an idiot, I took a 'steady' at that last fence.

24. "*I felt I had the race won . . . what a mistake.*"

What a mistake. I knew it instantly for almost at the moment of landing I was passed and my rival, ridden by Dermot Daly, went on to win by half a length or so. Dismounting I gave *Leopard* a real pat, saying 'Sorry old boy, it was my fault, I was a fool.' I cursed myself silently and at the same time thanked my stars that nothing worse had happened. Years later when I read Anna Karenina and came to the famous race episode, where Vronsky makes an error at the last jump and breaks his horse's back, I remembered how comparatively lucky we'd been.

Sunday for *Leopard* couldn't be his usual day of rest and he was curious about all the hustle and bustle. The bands playing as several Regiments swung off to Church Parade, nothing unusual about that, but the Riding School doors were wide open. He could see men in brown canvas fatigue dress washing down the walls, the windows, frantically polishing those giant mirrors. Looking glasses indeed! How often had *Leopard* stolen a sly sideways glance and thought 'My what a chap I am.'

Now a lorry had stopped outside, piled with what looked like grass — surely the School wasn't going to be turned into a field? No, but the turf was carefully unloaded and fitted together and gradually a fine lawn grew around the school. By the time it had all been rolled it looked fit for the pitch at Lords or Wimbledon's Centre Court. Two more lorries rolled up, laden with flower tubs, dark green with yellow hoops, and these they placed judiciously by the entrance and down the length of the walls. Yet another lorry arrived, alight with perfect daffodils, shrubs and scarlet polyanthus, all in pots. They planted the pots in those gaily painted tubs. 'Ah,' thought *Leopard,* he had got it at last. Very knowingly and confidentially he whispered to *Cully* and *Flying Fish* that this, of course, was a Flower Show , 'like those we've seen at Agricultural Shows, you know — perhaps the blooming bulls, cows, pigs and the like will turn up soon.' The work went steadily on. White posts appeared, edging the lawn, a thick white rope joining them. But no livestock, not even an old sheep arrived.

What transfiguration! With the great doors being painted

as a final touch that gaunt Riding School of ours shone as colourful and festive-looking as the Royal Pavilion and Members Tents at Ascot.

Dusk drew in, lights came on, the busy men fell out, work completed. And what work! Would this Riding School always remain so immaculate, or was it one more example that the soldier is a notable perfectionist if it comes to production.

Next day when they entered *Leopard* tossed his head in acknowledgement: all as perfect inside as out. More daffodils, polyanthus, even tulips rose in the corners and turf decorously bordered the school's arena. That dull old balcony was now a bank of flowers, with a green carpet and comfortable chairs. Something must be 'on'. Oh yes, indeed, but just precisely what? And then he heard Peat chattering away with Turnbull and caught 'Thank goodness the old boy is well . . .' 'Old, eh? Huh, well it wasn't my fault I lost on Saturday and I'd like to know what's expected of me now, old as I am'. *Leopard* grumbled on in this vein for a little while and then forgot about it.

Later, everyone in the stable listened while Peat said in his broad Yorkshire, 'This is what's called a Command Performance, a Royal Command Performance, for the King has indicated that the Queen, the Princess Royal and His Majesty wished to see the now famous four horses and three small ponies of the 5th Inniskilling Dragoon Guards. Time has had to be allowed for this during His Majesty's tour of the troops. So look to it.'

That Monday and Tuesday only our stars were permitted to use the School. For the tournament horse and rider who would be great the watchword should be 'Practise, practise then more practise'.

Only *Leopard*, *Gertie*, *Greasy* and *Red Lady* were to perform, for fifteen minutes. Apart from the little ponies and *Jerry* of course. But *Leopard* had decided to accept them, a trifle grudgingly perhaps.

The day, 'the' day arrived — and such a beautiful one. The Royal Route lined by troops, swords drawn, the band in full dress with shining helmets, red and white plumes and scarlet tunics.

Four Daimler's drew up. *Leopard* and his friends out of sight could hear the band playing the Royal Salute. Our quartet of course was waiting in the wings, trying to control their nerves. The pumping of the heart, the slight sweat, the fear. As any prominent actor will tell you, no performer can escape those symptoms — and the more famous and experienced you are the worse it gets.

Despite the theatrical aspect this was to be no 'fancy dress' affair. Spick and span, but not the ultimate in formality. So

25. *"Four Daimlers drew up."*

the arena party appeared in their green trousers and singlets, while the riders waited in their blue tunics with chains on the shoulders and white cross belts and green breeches with broad primrose stripe.

At last the call came and we entered in single file, led as always by *Leopard*. We formed up and saluted their Majesties. Off with those glittering double bridles, no need for them. The Band struck up and turn by turn reeled off the familiar tunes. Only the best of the turns, time was short, finishing as we jumped the flames of those tall candles.

Leopard watched gravely as Rushton and his tiny ponies swept on. But how the King laughed!

The trumpeters had their final flourish, the cymbals crashed and our display was over. A moment's silence, the four of us sitting very still until I gave the order. *'Gloves off'* (One glove off). *Make much of your horses. One, one two! Gloves on!'*

Each of the four riders saluted. The band played the *'Royal Salute'*, and then the regimental March, *'Fare Ye Well Inniskilling'*. I knew, indeed know, the words by heart and they sang in my head that day as we stood fast.

> *A lady of honour, of fame and renown,*
> *A gentleman's daughter of Monaghan town;*
> *As she rode by the barracks, the beautiful maid,*
> *She saw from her coach our Dragoons on parade.*
> *They were dressed all as gaily as gentlemen's sons;*
> *And their bright shining blades, and their carabine guns,*
> *And their brass-mounted pistols she noted full soon,*
> *For her love was a bold Inniskilling Dragoon.*
> *"Oh bright son of Mars, you that stand on the right,*
> *Your arms shining out like the stars of the night,*
> *Oh Willie! Dear Willie! you've 'listed too soon,*
> *To serve as a brave Inniskilling Dragoon."*
> *"Oh Flora' Dear Flora! your pardon I crave!*
> *'Tis now and for ever that I am your slave;*
> *But your parents upbraid you from morning till noon*
> *For loving your true Inniskilling Dragoon."*
> *"Oh Willie! Dear Willie! don't mind what they say!*
> *Sure maidens must ever their parents obey.*
> *When the foe you are fighting they'll soon change their*
> *   tune*
> *And cry, 'God send you safe, Inniskilling Dragoon"*
> *"Farewell, Inniskilling! Farewell for a while*
> *To all our fair waters and every green isle!*
> *When the war's at an end we'll turn home again soon,*
> *And they'll welcome the bold Inniskilling Dragoon."*

We'd a few years left yet. A breeze had got up and clouds must have been racing for as the band reached the last few bars, several shafts of sunlight pierced the windows, lighting the school at different points, picking out the tulips, the daffodils, the patches of grass. One of those almost unbelievable miracles when nature seems to applaud some occasion in our lives, striking awe in our hearts.

26. *"Our display was over."*

CHAPTER 14
The Coronation, 1937

Winter passed and *Leopard* saw little of his master. Peat explained that he'd gone to some place in France, somewhere called Saumur, where he'd learn more about riding. *Leopard* thought that odd indeed and tried to puzzle out how he, *Leopard,* could possibly learn anything more, let alone his master.

Two new companions had arrived, one pale cream with a white mane and tail, called *Peroxide,* the other, *Shannon Priest,* a black like those he'd seen in the London barracks. They had come from over the sea, from Ireland. 'Mm, foreigners' muttered *Leopard* to himself.

His master returned in March. Waiting to go to the Riding School one morning, *Leopard* was having a little munch, not wanting to be interrupted, when I appeared with a number of strangers. But who were these lean figures in their black boots and breeches, their black tunics and gold buttons? *Leopard* eyed them warily. Yes, strangers all right, and the talk sounded odd: rapid and yet very light, like the merest touch of a whip at the gallop. Then he caught the word Saumur — Ah! so these were the men from that sinister place which had imprisoned his master for so long, these were the sombre Instructors! 'Just you wait' thought *Leopard,* 'We might teach you a thing or two.' He swallowed.

A little later *Leopard* gave his display, with the master aboard and without a bridle, of course. I chatted a little with the Men in Black, then dismounted and — *Leopard* could hardly believe it — one of them stepped forward and mounted him. Our hero didn't quite bare his teeth, but he did in his mind, thinking 'You watch out, Mr. Instructor.'

Leopard did exactly what he wanted, determined to show that he couldn't be ridden without a bridle by just anyone. He cantered around, took the odd fence and when he felt like it gave a buck or two, but he had to admit his rider was perfect — there might only have been a feather in the saddle.

When I called *Leopard* to me for a handful of oats his rider sat and laughed and laughed while his comrades chaffed him about his bucking bronco, until my dear horse felt a nudge under the elbow: of course, he understood my signal and promptly lay down in the tan. The young officer's smart uniform wasn't quite so smart when he extricated

27. *". . . without a bridle of course."*

himself but he took it in good part and his companions gave a hearty cheer. No hard feelings and he slipped *Leopard* a lump of sugar and a friendly pat as Peat led him away.

An itinerant life that year, more than usual. We went to Belfast, and *Peroxide,* his new pale cream pal, showed him round his home town; we travelled to Jersey. One day as winter began to close in *Leopard* heard Peat and Turnbull cursing a bit — 'Just when we're starting to really get to know a . . . place we . . . well have to leave the . . .: they tell us a . . . soldier must follow the . . . drum . . . it. Oh well, at least Colchester sounds like a good . . . spot. We'll be the only Cavalry Regiment there, that'll be nice, you'll get better 'unting and you'll all like that. Boss is giving up the Trick Ride and taking over command of a squadron . Not so competitive a life but better wait and see, lads, he may find somat new for us all.'

The trundling rail journey was of a sort *Leopard* now recognised shunting off at angles in a circle on the outskirts of London — or so it seemed. At Colchester station to his mild surprise they moved off in a self-contained party of five, the family so to speak — *Fish, Peroxide, Shannon, Priest, Teddy* and himself, shepherded by Peat, Luxford and Turnbull — and they passed without pause through the barracks and on. Where could they be aiming for? A mile or more beyond they turned through a rather magnificent gate past the facade of a large, apparently empty house and into — oh wonder! — what can only be described as a Palace of the Horse Heaven. The sun shone on that yard as though it always would, on the fresh paint work and well raked gravel. There were ten loose boxes and a line of stalls and the old brass fittings shone like gold in ancient Constantinople. *Leopard* had by now learned to recognise his name and there, sure enough, it stood out on his door, picked out in yellow shadowed with green, in true signwriter fashion. Turnbull, Peat and Luxford were to live in a little cottage attached to the stable block overlooking this yard fit for a King, and here peace would reign, no clatter of accoutrements, no running orderlies, no trumpet call at dawn.

115

Berechurch Hall had been the home of some powerful 'squire' not so long before, with a full house of hunters and carriage horses in these stables. We seemed to stand at an intersection of time with change pushing on fast at our heels. I won't say we were aware of it exactly but we were certainly determined to enjoy ourselves while we could.

Leopard wished 'Long may this last'. A day came when he was introduced to a very attractive lady, and while his virtues were sung the lady patted and stroked him appreciatively and drew on an inexhaustible variety of titbits. Lulled in his bower of bliss *Leopard* could not believe his hearing when the master said, '*Leopard,* this lady and I are going to get married: you will of course always be with us, but we may have to move again.'

'Not again!' *Leopard* suppressed a soldierly groan, but later *Fish* pointed out that they wouldn't be doing so badly if that beautiful lady fulfilled her promise as a supplier of titbits. Agreed, and so no grumbles when Peat explained shortly afterwards, 'The boss has got married, we're off again, and let's hope we stay there for a bit!'

I should love to know what *Leopard* really thought of Wakes Hall, overlooking a valley nobly wooded with ash and oak and a narrow brook curling at the bottom. There was a farm behind the stables with one particular paradise for my horse — acres of green peas. *Leopard* found it just too easy to grab a quick mouthful, but, fortunately, Mr. Percival had plenty and he loved horses.

In the early hours of Summer mornings *Leopard* was exercised in those five hundred acres. In the fields the master gathered mushrooms and then, almost wandering it seemed, beside the flag irises, while partridges whirred away at his approach, the meadow-sweet cloaking many a mallard and then on, into the woods carpeted with late primroses where the pheasants lived, and even a fox.

More like my dear Yorkshire, *Leopard* probably thought, but rather here than foggy Fulford Barracks! Training as ever, but touches of luxury appeared: no eight mile ride to barracks for a motor car and large hórse trailer took them in style. Yes, a happy horse life, and whenever *Leopard* noticed the clouds gathering and approaching he certainly never thought of war.

Here we must insert a solemn historical note. Although two Regiments had already given up their horses, wisdom had prevailed with the Army Council and despite calls for economy, Officers were allowed to keep a horse or two, as it was considered, rightly, that hunting and polo were essential elements in the training and fitness of a Cavalry Officer. There were no substitutes. You cannot develop an eye for the country nor the ability to make decisions in a tank, no matter how well equipped it was. That such traditional cavalry training fortified our officers, was fully demonstrated in the Middle East and subsequently in France. Our horses helped to give us a nice life too, but you always pay for pleasant things at some time.

That Spring of 1937 *Leopard* began to notice there were far fewer of his kind in barracks. Lorries he knew and accepted but what about those lopsided monsters with retreating foreheads, skidding so swiftly in their rattling chains? They filled him with foreboding as some nightmares do. 'April is the cruellest month' a poet said, and in that month *Leopard* watched the Band play while soldiers armed with tin cans and bearing flags formed up in two lines. Most of the few remaining horses moved between the lines, the men shouted, banged their tins, waved the flags. What could it mean? He'd seen that sort of lark with Police Horses competing at Horse Shows, but Cavalry Horses, trained to fight? No enemy used tin cans.

Peat marched jauntily into the stables one morning later that month, saying, 'Come on, lad, no racing this year, we're off to London, so we must smarten you up a bit — the boss is going t'Coronation. Ay, you'll see our new King and Queen.

Like all horses, *Leopard* had a good memory: his image of London was a lovely green park which he recognised through the side window of his trailer, but surprisingly they passed the barracks and in through an imposing stone gate. Leading him out Peat whispered in his ear, 'This here is Tattersalls, where they sell horses and ponies — but never you worry, our master would never sell you.'

At least a hundred smart horses were comfortable in stalls with plenty of good clean straw and gradually *Leopard* realised that his master, Mike Ansell, was in charge of them all. Early morning exercise they had for they'd been engaged to transport generals and the like — who seldom rode a horse — and the horse must be kept calm. Imagine the calamity if equine mischief made it irresistible for one or more of them to give a buck and unseat high ranking officers or Dignitaries of the Empire in the procession!

As May 12th, Coronation Day, drew nearer more and more horses crowded in until Tattersalls was about to burst. To his horror, *Leopard* saw tents and 'lines' going up on his green grass — how awful if it rained! Of course it did, so that he could see neither grass nor bulbs for the mud. Thank the Lord it stopped and with lashings of soap and water you could almost hear the scrubbing throughout Piccadilly, until the horses of the Royal Scots Greys in particular stood out dazzling in the sombre dawn. Troopers made sure there would be no more rolling in that delightful mud!

When *Leopard* stood waiting at eight on the Day, with shining brass head dress, bosses on the bridle and stirrups, that huge bit adorned with the Regimental crest, and I too appeared in full dress, he thought, 'I do hope there'll be plenty of people to see me.' He need not have feared, for already they were ten deep along the five mile route but he hadn't quite realised that with the duties as Marshal, his Master had the privilege of moving up and down the columns of troops. *Leopard* gazed and was gazed on, he fancied by men in Scarlet, Sky Blue, Navy Blue and even Green tunics and twenty-five Bands spaced along the route, the crowds cheering and clapping. *Leopard* asked himself why, chewing his ornamental bit, wasn't life always like this? With helmets, plumes and cockades, with cuirasses casting back the sunlight, swords drawn, with trumpets calling and drum pounding and there, look! The Glass Coach had arrived and this was no Fairy Tale! For life should always be a celebration, a Coronation, a Fête, a Feast Day, with dancing, singing, joy everlasting and Their Majesties bearing down on us in their great coach drawn by eight perfect greys!

Big Ben gave us eleven strokes and after his burst of emotion *Leopard* was glad of a short pause — and felt peckish. Had his master forgotten our secret store in the wallets under the dark blue saddle cloth with its gold edging? No, the ration of 'marching' chocolate and sugar appeared. We shared that as we rode along the columns. Many parts of this London — for there are several Londons — *Leopard* had not seen: the Embankment, the dark slow river, Nelson on his soaring column, a noble flight of steps with a Duke of York, also very aloft. *Leopard* felt a little anxious that they had a perch so high.

He had even less sense of time than is common to a horse that day. Chimes from the Abbey rang their sequences, signifying to the Nation an end to that most exhalting of services. Four Troopers of the Life Guards led the Procession, those Guards Charles II had formed from his attendant Cavaliers in exile, down Whitehall, past where his father Charles I was executed, up a Regent Street 'Prinny' would be surprised to see, along an Oxford Street where roaring crowds gave *Leopard* no chance to admire his peacock feathers in the plate glass windows, and where I would pass again, two years hence, in a light tank with the name *Leopard* painted on the turret, making my way to war.

CHAPTER 15
The end of an era

Mornings mean so much. Our best efforts. our beginnings. One in September of Coronation Year, *Leopard* and *Flying Fish* were saddled up as for war, nose-bags, picketing pegs and canvas water buckets slung all over them. The Trumpeter sounded to mount, then 'Walk March' and we were on the road to Buntingford. The last time a regular Mounted Squadron would go out' on manoeuvres in England. Fortunately *Leopard* didn't know that and when they camped he and the *Fish* amiably disported themselves in a large park. Good grass, rather different from the heather they used to crunch at Catterick. That was about eight years before. The men were the same, the general set-up almost the same, they still had rifles and swords but there were quaint innovations: two seater cars with wireless sets and masts. I can't be sure whether *Leopard* or I flippantly wondered where the sails were. However, it would save some luckless trooper having to gallop about with messages.

Towards the end of the week everyone in camp seemed a bit more agitated than usual. *Leopard* noticed some fierce looking gentlemen striding about with red bands round their caps. *Fish* murmured, 'Watch out, those are generals'. *Leopard* didn't know what to think and decided to wait on events.

Next morning, Peat bore down on them saying, 'Come on

Fish, my lad, the Captain's going to ride you this morning — *Leopard,* you'll be with me till evening.' That had a mysterious note but *Leopard* was by now prepared for surprises, proof that he'd become the complete soldier. The squadron moved off, *Leopard* twitching his nostrils in anticipation — perhaps there'd be a little excitement at last, he felt he deserved some compensation for being deprived of his racing!

They trekked a dozen miles, dismounted and swung into the familiar routine: saddles off, Peat's charges watered and fed, he strode away to his mug of tea and can of stew. Wouldn't we all have been paralysed if we had realised that our familiar motions, mere ordinary routine, were in fact drawing us to the end of a chapter?

Leopard observed his master, the Squadron Leader, near the little Austin motor cars, among a group of Officers all absorbed reading their maps. The wireless sets crackled away like mad. Something definitely 'on'. Peat was now back muttering to himself and *Leopard* and *Fish* certainly overheard — 'Hell, we'll be out for the night and looks like a wet one too: damn those aeroplanes . . .'

The call rang out: 'To Boot and Saddle'
There's no time now to think of your very best girl,
This may mean a spell to make you squirm and whirl,
See that the saddle is right,
See that your sword scabbard's tight,
Some day it may sound to fight!
When the day comes,
For the big guns,
See that you're there,
Doing your share —
Look alive! Saddle and boot!

Rain was already pelting and night's dark joined the clouds as the Squadron went off at a very fast trot, occasionally breaking into a canter. Somewhere ahead a hero, the Troop Leader 'Monkey' Blacker (later General Sir Cecil Blacker) with a sodden map guided them down the lanes and sometimes over ploughed fields. On and on, hardly a halt, *Leopard* trying not to think of drinks or meals. He longed to know if others needed to draw breath but all he knew was his master's voice, that relentless, 'Get on'. Shots in the distance, the hooded lights of the little cars and the nagging crackle of their wireless sets. 'Get on! Get on!' *Leopard* had long stopped thinking at all, too tired and too determined not to give in and then he felt his master's gloved hand gentle on his neck. He lifted his head and knew the dawn was breaking and the rain had gone. Now they closed up, moving more cautiously down a narrow lane: 'Dismount for Action'.

Leopard and his companions were swiftly led into a wood and soon he heard the dismounted Troopers firing, obviously an attack, but brief, for the order rapped out 'Stand Fast'. The Squadron Sergeant Major was back with orders to bring up the 'led' horses. When Peat arrived with *Leopard* close to his master they found a tremendous row going on. Those men with red hat bands seemed to be everywhere, some with white arm bands: one with a face redder than his hat band, tinged with blue, eyes starting like a bull frog's, argued furiously and with increasing desperation. Their master slipped over to *Flying Fish* and *Leopard* and gave them a good pat, saying under his breath, 'Well done — we've caught a Brigade Headquarters almost asleep!' *Leopard* didn't need to glance at his master to know that he was laughing, though he probably didn't show it.

Highly satisfactory. The umpires signified victory for the Inniskilling Squadron. They were tired but ready to go on despite the speedometers on the Austins showing a mileage of seventy-two covered in eleven hours that night. Not a horse dropped out, nor was a shoe lost thanks to Gus Newport, the Farrier Major and those who had worked under him. Gus Newport, later Major Newport, was awarded the M.B.E. for escaping from Crete.

Just before leaving the wood *Leopard* had noticed a large house at the end of the lane and thought wistfully of what lovely stables it might have. He was in luck, for his master had reasoned along similar lines: why go back to Buntingford when the Master of the Essex and Suffolk Foxhounds would welcome them here at Dunmow?

And so it was. Sun rewarded us for our labours that day and if Apollo looked in our direction — to see Peat, back comfortable against his saddle, placidly eating his rations, the horses resting, or Troopers cleaning their rifles, swords and saddlery, the well wooded land stretching in all directions, few sounds but the calls of birds and chatter of cricket's — he would have approved a scene unchanged for two hundred and fifty years.

I plotted our course for home — 28 miles — and when we'd gone to rest that night in the open. I lay awake for a long time. My thoughts and feelings were very confused: pleasure at our success in the manoeuvres, numbed by an indefinable uneasiness about the future, plus the certainty that my horses would never go to war and could never again take part in manoeuvres. I was glad of the first part of that certainty but not the second. I couldn't resolve the contradiction. Even when clouds drew covers over the stars I still couldn't get to sleep.

There's little more to tell. *Leopard* enjoyed that Autumn at Wakes Colne, then my home, in so far as anywhere can really be home for a soldier. Through January and February he exercised in that lovely country with his chums *Grand Slam* and *Peroxide*; two or three times a week they went for gallops at Berechurch. Berechurch, I don't like to recall the name. *Leopard* was scheduled to race at Tweseldown in the middle of March — a course he knew and liked well. Earlier in the month we went to Berechurch for our regular work

"My horses would never go to war and never again take part in manoeuvres."

28.

124

out. I mounted *Leopard,* he seemed happy and fit, and we settled to a fast steady canter for about a mile. Then he fell. I got up and even before I laid my hand on him I knew he was dead. I looked down. My sight blurred. I seemed to see through my dear horse the scene of our last night on manoeuvres. I could understand nothing and yet I did understand.

He died from a clot of blood reaching his heart, without pain. He had given everything to me. He gave everything to his Regiment, and just before the Army gave up their horses, *Leopard* gave up his life. It was right.

EPILOGUE

In that same March, 1938, the 5th Royal Inniskilling Dragoon Guards 'Trooped the Standard and Guidon' for the last time mounted. They yielded up those emblems they'd borne mounted for two hundred and fifty years. They would continue to ride as individuals, yes, but not as soldiers.

I was lucky. I was posted to York with a Yeomanry 'horsed' Cavalry Brigade and returned there with my horses, but not with *Leopard*. Like his father, *Maître Corbeau*, he had left those beautiful Wolds never to return.

29. *"Trooped the Standard and Guidon for the last time mounted."*

GLOSSARY

Bandolier. A belt worn over the left shoulder. It had nine pouches, five in front and four behind. In each pouch two clips of five rounds of ammunition were carried. Thus, in front 10 clips of five each — 50 rounds. The horse carried a second bandolier around his neck. This was a spare one, therefore each Trooper carried 180 rounds.

Cavesson. Head collar with a steel nose band on which are three rings. The lunge, or long rein, is attached to either of these.

Clinches. The shoe is nailed to the hoof of the horse and the tip of the nail is turned over and "clinches" the shoe to the foot. This is quite painless.

Cuirasse. Chest and back armour worn by the Household Cavalry on ceremonial occasions.

Puttees. Strips of material wound round the leg from ankle to knee, instead of boots, by all ranks below Sergeant Major when mounted.

Saumur. French Cavalry School founded about 1790. The instructors wear a black uniform with gold buttons and braid. This originated from the early days when many of the twelve instructors were exceptional civilian horsemen, who always wore black breeches, tail coats and top hats.

Standard and Guidon. Standards, scarlet emblazoned with the Regimental crests and Battle Honours, were carried by all Cavalry Regiments until 1744. From that year Dragoons carried Guidons. The Guidon was almost similar except it was a "fish tail" shape. Later, when the 5th Dragoon Guards and Inniskillings became amalgamated they only carried the Standard, combined in the two Regiments.

Strangles. A contagious disease of the nose and throat, sometimes fatal. Most common with young horses.

Weedon. The British School of Equitation, formed about 1920, when the Cavalry and Royal Artillery Equitation Schools were amalgamated. Weedon is almost in the centre of England, the situation being chosen by King George III for fear of invasion during the Napoleonic Wars as a safe refuge.

INDEX